image consultant | style coach | speaker | author

CONFIDENCE
is always in style

by Doreen Dove

ISBN-13: 978-0692304761 (Doreen Dove)
ISBN-10: 0692304762

Dedication

*In memory of my wonderful brother who always thought I was the bee's knees!
I know you would be very proud of me and I check in with you nightly as I gaze at the
Big Dipper, our special hangout!*

*To my own checklist of very important people who have inspired me to be the best
version of me! I cannot thank you enough. This book is a labor of love and is for all of you.*

*My parents who taught me the meaning of hard work, persistence, patience and hope.
My husband who always said to pursue this just for the love of it.
My daughters who constantly tell me I am still young and full of dreams and possibilities.
My best-girlfriends-forever who know me better than anyone - thanks for the daily inspirations.*

"I have always believed that fashion was
not only to make women more beautiful,
but also to reassure them,
give them confidence."
Yves Saint Laurent

TABLE OF CONTENTS

"I'll stop wearing black when
they make a darker color."
Wednesday Addams

STEP 6

Reintroduce

Lastly, reintroduce your garments to your closet in an intuitive fashion, left to right. Sleeveless, short sleeve, long sleeve silkies, long sleeve wovens, light-weight sweaters (they love the soft grip hangers and then are not a wrinkled mess when you go to wear them), and then jackets. All clothing should run white to black within each category.

The bottom bar will house pants running left to right – dress pants, casual pants, jeans (again white to black within those parameters). Then skirts – same theory!

Now add some lavender sachets and a fluorescent light if you do not have one. You need to be able to see what you are shopping for!

Your new system should make sense and make getting dressed everyday stress-free. If this is making you feel overwhelmed or uncomfortable, than it is time to get your closet some help. You'll see Closet Edit under my Services online, just reach out: I'm here for you!

CLIENT STORY

My client Anne had a travel schedule that even a pro tennis player would have trouble keeping up with. Suitcase empty, suitcase full, outgoing and incoming dry cleaning taking over her very precious home time and she really had no clue what she even had to choose from for her next trip. Her life was chaos, not to mention having two young children in the mix. It was painfully obvious that she needed a system. A system so she could know what she had, how to wear it, how to pack and dress in color capsules and how to control the dry cleaning/laundry chaos.

We started with a closet audit, editing, revising and setting it up by season - the season she lives in and the season she travels to. I carved out a dedicated area where her 'personals' that needed to travel with her each and every time were kept in one spot - passport, travel docs, phone chargers, travel makeup and toiletry bag and so on. When she returned from a trip she unpacked and left them there where they were waiting for her next excursion. No hunting and gathering needed. We made sure she had 2 of each wardrobe essential that she packed so there wasn't ever last minute dry cleaning or laundry drama - nude, white and black bras, black pants, crisp white shirt, dark wash jeans, comfortable airplane cardigan, etc. I also created a digital look-book of her wardrobe which includes, shoes, handbags and accessories, eliminating the 'how could I forget that syndrome'.

Just these few changes alone made a huge difference in her stress level.

CHAPTER 4

Wardrobe Essentials
What every woman needs

Client Story

One of my plus sized clients, Abby, only shopped in one store for 20 years. They only carried elastic waist pants. This was a woman in a position of power in a large firm. Despite her education and accomplishments, she was the least confident and most self-conscious woman in the room. Not because of her size; she is perfectly comfortable as a plus-size woman, but because of her clothing choices – elastic waist pants and drapey tops that were making her look larger than she was. What was holding her back was not knowing the 3 Must Have Ws.

W # 1: *You must know* Where to shop

I find the least stylish women are repeat shoppers – they shop in the same stores year after year, going down the same aisles, buying the same v-neck cashmere sweaters over and over. They have had the same look for 30 years – even family photos are pete and repeat. They are missing out on so many other potential great options. Styles, fits, fabrics, designers that they would look amazing in! I ask them to reverse their order down the aisles the next time they go to the grocery store and see how many new things end up in their cart. That's what can happen at the mall too!

W # 2: *You must know* What to buy

Shopping is painful for most – too many stores, too many things, too much schlepping and no one to help you once you are naked in the dressing rooms. Whew, I am exhausted just thinking about you! You cannot buy a new washer for the faucet unless you know what size and shape the faucet is. So first you need to know your size – we just went over that.

And your body profile – we touched briefly on that – this is where my expertise really kicks in. Trying things on you that you never would have glanced at and performing the search and find long before you enter the store. If you are shopping on your own, you could search online and check the online chat to see if it is in stock in the store before you even schedule a mall trip.

You have to know what you are looking for, so you need a list! In order to have a list, you need to know what you already have, and subsequently what is missing becomes your "to buy" list. Remember back to the closet edit conversation and build your list from there. Shop with a list so you know what to buy.

"Whoever said that money can't buy happiness, simply didn't know where to go shopping."
Bo Derek

W # 3: *You must know* What price to pay

Just because it is on sale, it doesn't mean you should own it. If you have your list, you can shop around by price. You can wait for a sale or a coupon. If you don't plan, you buy either the wrong thing or pay the wrong price. That's how you end up with one-shot wonders in your closet – lonely items with no mates!

You need to have a clothing budget. Most working women spend between $2000 and $3000 a year on clothing. That is $160 to $250 per month, mind you that includes clothing, shoes, jewelry, dry cleaning, the whole shebang. Create a budget, create a list, shop off-season when possible and shop with purpose. Plan the product, plan the mall, plan the store, the parking space, the price, the discounts or coupons! Plan, plan plan!

SHOP YOUR CLOSET

Before we get ahead of ourselves, let's stop and talk about the closet edit we just did. What you might see as the same old stuff in your closet from pants to blouses to jewelry, a trained eye will see as a wealth of possibilities. Your lifestyle might include dinner with your friends once a week, attending networking events, corporate meetings, supporting a non-profit, and even 10-day vacations. Does your wardrobe support your lifestyle?

When I mention these things, most of you are ready to throw all your old clothes out and start over. However, you would be really surprised at how many fabulous things are hiding in your closet.

Others have called me "the wardrobe whisperer" because I have a gift for unearthing one-shot wonders lost in the dark spaces of your closet and creating smashing outfits around them. However, now that you have become intimate with what you own, you just might be able to channel your own "stylist" creativity and create a list of what's missing!

Remember the food pyramid?
Apply those principles to your shopping list (variety, moderation, portion control) and you'll achieve a well-balanced wardrobe.

The Basics

Build a strong foundation with a strategic selection of basics that will mix with almost everything in your closet.

Blouses
We are talking feminine necklines to give a traditional business suit a pretty and modern spin, or paired with a cardigan and jeans to update a more casual look. Blouses are also a great way to add color and prints to an outfit. When everything else is neutral, let the blouse bring some personality into the picture. You will need that quintessential icon of style, a crisp white cotton blouse and it should be a non-iron shirt. I recommend an investment piece from Brooks Brothers that comes in 3 different styles, fitted, tailored and classic as well as regular and petite. Also invest in a few classic stripes.

Knitwear
Choose knitwear in natural fabrics like cotton, wool, and cashmere as they will wear better and hold their color longer than artificial fabrics. Cardigans, wraps and crew necks are great for layering and are a softer, more casual alternative to a blazer. Don't forget the all-important black fitted turtleneck!

A-line Skirt
This classic shape looks great on ANY body type. It defines the waist while flaring subtly from the hips. Women with fuller hips find the A shape helps to conceal them, while those with minimal hip action are thrilled to discover this shape actually accentuates them.

Pencil Skirt
Pencil skirts can flatter almost any body shape when chosen carefully. For the more androgynous figure, look for a straight and narrow cut to hug and accent the hips. If you are shapelier, look for one with a thicker waistband that falls straight from the hip. This will help to create balance in your bodyline while still showing off your curves. Versatility is key, as this skirt can go from the boardroom to dinner with a silk blouse and a few accessory changes.

Fitted Jacket
There is a reason corporate executives always wear suits to important meetings. There is something very "smart" about a fitted jacket. It can elevate even a pair of jeans and a T-shirt into a more pulled together ensemble. A structured jacket accents the waistline, while small shoulder pads can de-emphasize a larger chest and balance a fuller hip.

News flash – the 80's "Working Girl" shoulder pads are out of style. Even Oprah had a good laugh at her historical shoulder pad drama. If your jacket is styled with pads, make sure the actual sleeve head sits where it should, right at the edge of your shoulder bone. When you purchase the jacket, look at all the points that should fit properly or could use a bit of expert tailoring, such as how the neckline sits, whether the button placement is at a flattering stance, and whether the length of the sleeves actually expose your hands!

Tailored Trousers It is all about the fit. Not all pants are created equal! Pants are the hardest clothing item to fit, so you have to work at finding the right cut for your body. Options include, petite, regular, tall, mid-rise, high-rise, pleat front, plain front, narrow leg, wide leg, plain bottom, cuffed bottoms – yikes – where to begin? Begin with your tape measure! Measure your height, inseam, waist, hips, and thighs and then refer to the size charts online! Every major retailer has posted size charts on their website. Most stores now carry specific models in trousers every season. Do your homework before you ever walk in the store. Find the shape & fit best for your proportion and then invest in your neutrals (black, navy, brown, tan) in a year-round fabric.

Suit A pant or skirt suit is a fantastic addition to any working woman's wardrobe as they can be worn together or broken up, creating more options. If you can find one with both pants AND a skirt, even better! Purchase the "best fabric" you can afford for longer wear, and if the fit is not precise, invest in tailoring.

Wrap Dress: A dress that wraps at the smallest part of your waistline or a faux wrap dress with a defined, banded waistline will flatter most shapes. The dress that made Diane Von Furstenberg famous is as versatile as it is flattering. Wear it layered (best with thin fabric camisoles) for the office and alone with a great pair of heels for date night.

One is never overdressed or underdressed with a little black dress
Karl Lagerfeld

Little Black Dress (LBD): Almost always at the top of every "essentials" list, the Little Black Dress is most likely already in your closet. Don't think about it just for evening soirees, as it can be a staple of your work wardrobe as well. A simple sheath made of high quality fabric can pair terrifically with a cardigan or blazer and string of pearls for the office. Remove said cover up and switch up the pearls for a bold bangle, statement necklace and rockin' heels, and you are ready for a night on the town.

Cocktail Dress: Not to be confused with the little black dress, you should have one AMAZING dress in your closet that you can pull out for that night when you know you want to make an entrance. It is all about incredible fit, fabrics that drape and hug in all the right places, and knowing that when you have that all important event (charity gala, holiday party, wedding, college reunion, etc.) you have this stylish option waiting in your closet.

Pumps: Invest in kitten heels or one to two-inch heels. Closed toes are more professional and can be worn all year long. Start with black and nude and add color as you build your inventory. Higher heels lengthen the leg and define the calf muscle.

High Heels: Every woman should own at least one pair, probably black or nude. High heels can turn a day outfit into night, add height to the vertically challenged, make you stand straighter, and work your calf muscles creating gorgeous gams. Let's be honest here, high heels are sexy! For those worried about the discomfort of wearing heels, please realize not all heels are created equally. Believe it or not, some heels can be quite comfortable and the term "high" is different for everyone – it could be a 2, 3, or even a 4-inch heel.

Fashionable Flats: You cannot escape "flats" these days. They are available in every color, textured, shiny, embellished, and at every price-point possible. Grab a few pair to wear with your lean jeans, skirts or casual dresses, but make sure they make a style statement other than "I am wearing these because they are comfortable." Opt for the pointier version to elongate your legs! Make sure this is a flat that looks like you want to wear it, not like you need to wear it!

Leather Jacket: Leather jackets have moved beyond the young rebels who favored them in black motorcycle styles. They now come in a variety of shapes including trenches, blazers and bomber styles. Choose the one that best fits your own shape and lifestyle. Coming in a number of different colors, they offer up a subtle luxury for all ages. And if leather is out of your price-range, go for pleather – very few spectators will ever know the difference!

Trench Coats

It doesn't get much more timeless than a trench. While not quite "season-less", you will get many more months wear out of this coat, than any other in your closet. Trenches come in a variety of lengths; choose the one that works best with your shape. You can have fun with the traditional navy, beige, or black by adding colorful scarves and stylish belts giving an unexpected spin to the classic trench. And then of course accessorize it with a great looking umbrella and pop your collar high and mysterious.

Let's do a deep dive here:

The classic definition of a trench is a raincoat made of waterproof heavy-duty cotton gabardine, leather, or poplin with detailing such as a removable lining, raglan sleeves, ten-button double-breasted wide lapels, epaulettes, pockets that button close, wrist straps that buckle up and a storm flap. Whew, can we talk details? The trench could certainly overpower most female forms. So we must be extra careful to interview the raincoat before we just jump into the trenches with it.

Here are a few styling tips for shopping for a classic trench:

Look for tailored lines – don't buy a coat that overwhelms you. Try on several sizes and styles, including regulars and petites, before you hand over your credit card.

Avoid unusual colors – we are talking hot pink and lime here. Khakis and tans will easily assimilate into any wardrobe, so of course those are a safe bet. However, all your choices do not have to be in the khaki realm. Other members of the neutral zone such as navy, olive, eggplant, and even red will work nicely as well.

Let your personality shine in the details, with unusual buttons, trims, tailoring, and even color blocking.

Trenches can be bulky or slim – it all depends on the look you are going for and the weather conditions you are trying to ward off. The classic trench worn in the windy city of Chicago would not be what Floridians would shop for. Those of you in the lower digit climates might want to consider a removable liner. Shop carefully and look for a zippered option as buttons create extra little bumps and hard spots head to toe – no need for any more of those!

Budget wise – you can be all over the spectrum here, with the cream of the crop obviously being Burberry. If you are looking at the trench as one of your investment pieces, then by all means, take the plunge. A classic trench will travel with you for years, keep you warm and dry, bump up your image, and not to worry – that cost per wear will go down to next to nothing because you will wear it for decades.

trench coats...

If you are considering making that investment, be sure to buy an authentic trench! Steer clear of any obvious timely fashion details, like a current voluminous swing coat – who knows if twenty years from now you are going to want to own anything voluminous! Think ahead, think about potential body changes, and perhaps plan a bit of room to grow. I mean, you can't really plan what car you might be driving but landing in the driver seat with a full-on lined trench coat five years from now when the mommy van has been down sized to your dream Mini Cooper might be something to keep in mind.

However, the coat should not be shapeless. Be sure you have a substantial belt – a key detail in the trench. Decide if you are a belt-buckle type of woman or a tie-it-up gal.

Then there is the single or double-breasted decision. If you are petite and slight of frame, a well-proportioned, proper length coat in a double-breasted style will beef you up a bit and add shape. Be sure to cinch the waist to accentuate the hourglass proportion. If on the other hand you are petite and full-bodied, the double-breasted styling will add pounds to your frame. Choose the single-breasted here.

Be sure to treat your raincoat with respect. It is shocking how few times women dry clean their coats. When you think about it, it really should be cleaned more often that you dry clean your dresses! It is the barrier between you and your morning coffee on the commuter train, the unspeakable things you might sit on in the subway, the unpredictable weather elements, and oh yes, don't forget the oils from the back of your neck as you pop the collar Pink Panther style!

When you make an investment in a classic trench, you must take care of it properly so it can take care of you.

"After rebranding our company, I realized that I needed rebranding. My wardrobe had not been updated in years and didn't reflect the emerging identity of the business. I needed to ramp up my professional image and didn't know where to begin. I had several important public events coming up and realized that I had nothing appropriate to wear. In three hours Doreen helped me to assemble everything I needed for a coordinated, professional wardrobe that fit my body type, taste, personality, work needs and budget. This whole experience has had a very positive impact on my work life." YA

CHAPTER 5

Got Challenges?
Let's talk solutions and fine tuning

Let's be honest, within the essentials listed in the previous chapter there are a few categories that require a bit more intervention, patience, and creativity.

Foundation Issues: We are talking boobs, bellies, butts, bunions, and bags!

The Boobs (also known as the Girls)

Now ladies – we are carrying around assets under our tops – and assets need to be insured! Insure the 'girls' with the best fitting bra you can afford. As Oprah exposed (pun intended) eight out of ten women are wearing the wrong size bra. Why is that? Would you walk around in the wrong size shoe?

Are your girls smashed into some bra that is too tight causing the dreaded side boob? Get your boobs, all four of them (if you count overflow), over to a top notch department store for a proper measurement by their Bra Fit Specialists. A well fitting bra will benefit you by giving you better posture, a perkier, younger looking chest, a classier look in your clothing, the appearance of a flatter and longer stomach and reduced back pain by locking and loading them where they are supposed to be.

Women strive for wardrobe perfection in their outerwear, but it all starts with proper fitting foundations. And did you ever hear of purging bras (not burning bras)? Women keep holding on and on, stacking them higher and higher in the drawer. I am reminded of our local mattress huckster who shows up on TV twenty times a day reminding us that our mattresses might be as old as Fenway Park. I think the better question would be "How old is the bra you are wearing today?"

CLIENT STORY

There is one thing that there is no shortage of in my business - women in the wrong size bra! What is with that? As I said earlier, would you wear the wrong size shoe? Case in point. I started working with a virtual client. Despite being virtual, she was subjected to my usual question, "Are the girls locked and loaded?" She had sent along the required selfies, and therefore, I had to ASK! Her response, oh certainly! Hmmm...maybe not so much. She admittedly had a bit of side boob going on. So I sent her off to Nordstrom on her lunch hour to meet with their extremely qualified bra fitters. I received a text an hour later with a selfie (can we say 'not advised') of the girls, lifted, locked and loaded. They were not in the original 36DDD but a 34G! Did you even know they had G's? I didn't and neither did she. Sometimes you really do need to outsource your style!

You should be fit for a bra every six months, okay, okay, once a year at least! Weight gain or loss of even just five pounds may change the fit of your bra. And for those of you with bigger assets, there are bigger fit challenges that go along with that.

If the bra band is too big, your bust will droop. If you don't have enough coverage in the cup you'll have breast overflow, which results in triple boob syndrome.

Your bra band should be parallel to the floor, low and snug on the back, not hanging off your neck. The cup of the bra should contain all your breast tissue and shouldn't pinch, bind, bite, or annoy. You want your breasts to be lifted, contained, and happy!

When you zero in on the best fitting bra, buy white, nude, and black.

The Bellies (Also known as Fuller-in-the-Middle)

With the "girls" now in place don't even think about smashing them into flatness by wearing the wrong style shaper! Yes, you just might need a shaper for the midsection. Many of us are having issues not just in the front tummy area but the dreaded back fat as well. Who wants to see that!

Look for a shaper that scoops under the bra so the now shapely boob-ettes can stand tall and proud. The shaper shapes the back and the stomach area under your bra-line. They can tuck into your pants or skirt also eliminating the dreaded muffin-top!

Remember my mantra – accentuate the assets (that would be the girls) and disguise the liabilities (that would be the front/back bubbles).

The Butts (No Ifs, Ands, or "Butts" about it)

The dreaded butt "V". Remember ladies – you have to look good when you leave the room – so no panty lines! People watch you longer as you walk away because there is no eye contact that forces them to stop staring! So leave your granny panties in the drawer with your other "drawers". Pop on a lower trunk shaper. Mind you, they are not like the old girdle days or even the original Spanx days where they were so tight our legs turned blue from lack of circulation. Now you can look good and still eat dinner! They have high tops and high thighs, low tops and long thighs. There is just about any shape in shapewear these days that will fit your unique shape!

So take all of your lingerie OUT of the drawer and do an honest assessment for fit. Purge the ill-fitting, worn out, downright ugly items.

We are going to stay on your butt for a bit, and talk about finding the best fitting pair of pants possible. I hear a collective groan out there right now. Don't despair, we are going to teach you how to interview the pants before you get naked with them in the dressing room.

Interviewing the Pants

Remember the 20 pairs of black pants you threw out in your closet edit? Let's avoid growing that stack again in the future.

Shopping for pants is like a first date. First, interview the pants and then get naked (well maybe)! Got your attention? Good…now pay attention! If you are going on a first date…what are the requirements you might have for the prospect? Let's pick 4: He's wearing a belt, he has change in his pockets, his pants aren't dragging on the floor, his butt isn't sagging in his Dockers.

Oh my, you are particular aren't you? If only you were that particular when it came to the choices that actually affect your pants!

Let's visualize the process of hunting, gathering, finding a dressing room, and then getting naked in the hopes of exiting said dressing room looking like Cate Blanchett in a perfect fitting, traffic stopping pair of pants!

Guess what – your chances of that happening if you have skipped the all-important interview process are nil, none, and zip! Plus – didn't your mother ever warn you about getting naked on the first date?
So what's the point? Let me help you with some "gathering" pointers – I call it the 4-point checklist.

Point #1

When is the last time you wore a belt? 10 years ago? Then why are you still buying pants with belts? Put those pants back on the rack!

Point #2

Do you have a little extra in the hips? Then why are you still buying pants with pockets? Note to self…there are no more phone booths so no need for jingling change in your pockets which translates to no need for pockets. Put those pants back on the rack!

Do you find you have a baggy butt in your pants? Then why are you buying pants with bottoms that are 12 inches wide? Do the math...12 inches, times two sides, equals 24 inches of fabric that actually starts at the hip! No wonder you have a baggy butt! Look for pants that have an 8 to 10-inch bottom, no wider unless you are going for the 70's look. Put those pants back on the rack!

Did I mention Dockers? Geez ladies; leave those stiff cotton pants for the guys! They can stand on their own – you don't even have to be wearing them! You need to be wearing your clothing as opposed to your clothing wearing you! Look for luxury fabrics like ponte knits, all season tropical wools, and blended fabrics that include a bit of Lycra for "forgiving" – anything but stiff cotton khakis that look like you are wearing your canvas boat bag. Put those pants back on the rack!

The long and short of it: Shopping can be challenging! Don't make it worse by hunting and gathering for the wrong thing and then dropping your drawers resulting in a huge, frustrating waste of time! Plus now you are naked in the dressing room with not a salesperson in sight. That's helpful!

Here's another pointer – shop online before you ever start the car! Take your measurements, match them up with the 'store fits' before you even step foot in the store. Most stores now carry at least four different styles to accommodate women's fabulous figures including petite, plus, long, high rise, low rise, slim, curvy and extra curvy. You can pre-shop online and then either buy there or call ahead to the store to make sure they have inventory.

The Bunions (Thank you Grandma)

What's your first memory of your feet going bad? I hear a collective sigh right now, which actually brings me comfort knowing I am not alone (misery loves company). What's your first memory of your grandmother? Here's mine, a trifecta of sorts: She had the softest skin, she collected salt and pepper shakers from around the world (despite never having left Rhode Island) and she had the ugliest shoes – ever! I did inherit soft skin, don't have a clue where the salt & pepper shakers went after an ugly family dispute (everyone has a crazy uncle), and damn, I refuse to wear the ugly shoes.

Here is my first memory of my feet going bad. I was sixteen years old, standing in the window as a model at Ann Taylor, and after 5 hours of mannequin-like posing I wanted to just stick a fork in my eye! Fast forward to the era of Pappagallo shoes – any Bostonians remember the Pappagallo Store on Newbury Street? Basically all the shoes looked the same – pumps, pumps, and more pumps. Wear those forty hours a week, and even a five year old would develop bunions.

Yes, I said the word that most can't spell – B-U-N-I-O-N-S. Where do they even come from? It's like my toes have become fingers and I am holding up the number five like a spread eagle!

My rock-bottom moment? When I was working in Manhattan as a buyer with six million dollars to spend in the market (you'd think with that kind of change, I could buy a shoe store) and I found myself at the end of a 10-hour day, thirty blocks from my hotel, and oh…did I mention it was raining? Been to NYC? When it rains the cabs disappear – quite the phenomenon.

What's a bunion girl to do? You got it… I hobbled barefoot back to the hotel and hoped the doorman had a bucket of lime for me to rinse my feet in before proceeding to the bar to deaden the senses.

So that's my story – what's yours? Here are a few quotes from my client questionnaires; if you recognize your quote, no worries – you still remain anonymous – but now you know you are not alone!

The Question: Do you have any foot or shoe challenges?
The Responses:
I have a large bunion on my right foot – do they sell shoes in 2 different sizes?
My feet are size 11 narrow – yikes!
Wide front foot and boney narrow heel and boney, boney (lots of boney here) ankles, high arch, low threshold to pain – whew!
High arches – cannot wear flat shoes…
Flat feet – cannot wear high arches…
I am extra curvy – even my feet…

Must I continue? As I've mentioned, my issue is of course HUGE bunions – ugly as hell. I considered moving to the North Pole so I could wear boots twelve months of the year, but alas, very few clients up there are concerned with their wardrobe image, so here I stay.

"Fashion is the armor to survive the reality of everyday life."
Bill Cunningham

bunions...

Here are a few tips & tricks – we are going to focus on shoes that are at the very least a bit fashionable here! We all know the ugly boxes we can find, but let's try to bump it up from my grandmother's shoes.

Shoe "fittings" are just like clothing "fittings". You must buy to accommodate the largest part of the foot and then "tailor" from there. (Similar to buying a jacket where you have to fit for the shoulders, and then perhaps have the waist tucked in or the sleeves shortened.) Shoe widths are available in wide and double wide! You can actually search online at stores like Zappos by width, size, color, price, arch support, heel height, and even wide-calf for boot season! We could go on for days with the "options by issues" but for the sake of space let's talk bunions.

If bunions are your issue, then go for the wide size to accommodate the "curves". Look for a shoe with an adjustable back strap so you can secure the heel.

Pay the piper – your feet will thank you! Consider that you might buy six pairs of inexpensive, un-comfortable flats this season, then rethink the plan and invest in one pair that will last for years and give your feet the respect they deserve!

Here's an extra comfort tip! If buying closed back shoes, use heel grips to keep your heels comfortably secure.

The Handbags

I am presuming that during the Closet Edit you trashed that out-of-date bag so let's just dive into what to buy to replace what you are now crying over. Women hate to part with handbags, something about holding on to 'baggage'. Let me set you straight – here is how to shop with purpose for your replacement handbag.

Shopping for the right bag can be painful. Totes, hobos, clutches, satchels, cross-bodies, messengers, duffles, and more, where's a girl to start?

Start where you most likely start each day – in the mirror! You must try bags on to make sure they fit! I mentioned to someone that I was writing about handbags today and she said, "I love my handbags – they always fit!" After I chuckled, I realized that that is not always the case.

"Is your closet overflowing but you still don't have anything you really want to wear? Doreen to the rescue! She will unearth buried treasures in your closet, help you say goodbye to clothes you haven't worn in years and never will again, and give you shopping suggestions to fill in wardrobe gaps that will help you identify and refine your personal style, all within your budget. In addition to her fashion expertise, Doreen brings a big smile and a positive can-do attitude. It's great therapy. You will actually be excited to decide what to wear the next day." JD

Shopping for Handbags

Here are some tips to ponder

Let's consider what a day in the life of your bag might entail. Placed on the seat of the car or forced to the floor? Placed on the hook in the bathroom or gripped like cash while you use the facilities? Thrown in a file drawer at the office or nicely displayed on your desk as a status statement?

Would you like your bag to be proudly standing and waiting for you so you can easily reach in and find your priceless things lined up in an orderly fashion? Would you like said bottom of bag to stay relatively clean? Then consider grommets on the bottom of your bag.

Are you looking to spend an arm and a leg on one bag and carry it everyday for the next decade to get your cost per wear down? Or are you looking to have a few bags so they actually can be styled along with your seasonal outfits?

Choosing a handbag is not to be taken lightly. Speaking of weight, you need to consider the weight of the empty bag before you add your 40 pounds of stuff. Just ask your mail carrier how painful it is to haul around a bag that is too heavy.

Handles

Do you like the straps lopped over your shoulder or do you prefer the hand straps? Remember you still have to carry your latte stylishly.

Are you large breasted? If so, let's skip the dreaded cross-body boob splitter. Ever owned a bag that the handles fall off the shoulder? I do – it's totally annoying – it's like a full time job configuring the handles. I wish I had read this book before purse shopping. When bag shopping, try them on with and without your coat. Be sure if it is a shoulder bag it will fit over your jacket when the weather requires outerwear!

Size

Buy a bag that is in proportion to your figure. The right bag can accentuate your assets – the wrong bag – well we all know that will accentuate the liabilities!

Are you tall and thin? Then buy rounded or slouchy. If you are curvy, opt for rectangular or sleek. Think the three bears: too small, too big, just right. Too small = no place for your stuff. Too big = the need to pile in more stuff. Just right = lots of benefit to that! The right size and style can knock pounds and years off your frame!

Color

Buying a classic bag? Consider buying basic colors, but incorporating a bit of color blocking! Consider combos such as black and navy, brown and tan, or gray and cobalt. Color blocking has been the rage for years now – keep up ladies, it is not just for clothing but also for shoes and handbags as well. Think versatile, but also think pop of color! Your purse is a great place to make a fashion statement.

handbags...

Never buy a purse without compartments. Trust me, you need them! Heres' proof, dump everything out onto the counter (this could be scary). Line up your bag essentials, items you carry everyday such as your wallet, phone, glasses, makeup bag, keys, pens, notepads, bottle of wine, etc. Now envision being in a store and your phone rings or you need your glasses to sign your American Express card. How long would it take you to find those items in a slouchy hobo bag, in a satchel, in a cross-body? Your bag needs to be purchased with the contents in mind. Kind of like having the kids in mind when you buy a car (well not quite, but close).

Be sure your bag stays upright when you put it down as opposed to flopping over like a rag doll. And be sure it has zippers or clasps for security – can you spell pickpocket?

Quality

Seriously, what do you hold more often than your bag? Go for the more expensive bag – you are worth it. Plus how many times have I preached about cost per wear? Say you pay $200 for a bag and use it for one season, half a year, a/k/a 182 days a year. Okay I'll do the math for you. $200 divided by 182 equals $1.09 per day. How much do you pay for your morning latte? Pay the $200 for the bag!

Shop for known brands like Cole Haan, Coach, Tory Burch, etc., and opt for leather and grommet bottoms to keep it clean. Check the stitching and seams for quality craftsmanship.

Scale

When it comes to scale, the size of the bag should be in proportion to your frame. If you are tall or fuller-sized, you don't want to be carrying a teeny-weeny bag – that makes you appear larger. If you have a tiny frame, carrying a large slouchy bag will overwhelm you. Now that we have taken care of boobs, bellies, butts, bunions, and bags, let's get down to some real shopping!

The Black Story

Pop of color galore! If you had just come across this jacket on the rack you might have turned and ran! What the heck do you do with a Kelly green jacket, other than win a golf tournament? Here's the answer, pair it up with your black foundational pieces. To make it a bit less conservative I finished the outfit with a statement necklace that brought in mixed metals and a few additional colors. This jacket would also look fabulous with a dark wash jean, a crisp white shirt and a sassy belt.

Remember, you must look good
when you leave the room!

CHAPTER 6

How To Become A Savvy Shopper
And look good doing it

HITTING THE SALES

Ready to take the plunge? Here are my tips for surviving the sales:

THE OUTLET MALL

Outlet shopping seems passé with the onslaught of online shopping, but alas dear readers, retailers are not going to take the time to list an item online when they only have a few pieces left. This however, is the benefit of the outlet excursion – one Prada bag at 70% off is not going to show up on the Saks 5th Ave website, but it will show up in the Saks Off 5th outlet store! So it might be worth making that annual trek out to suburbia in search of fabulous finds.

Here are several tips that can make your trip a bit less painful.

Plan your Strategy
Make a plan and stick to it so you can shop with purpose!

Plan the Products

As much as you might want to add that fabulous new bit of frosting to your wardrobe, first make sure the cake is ready! Check your bras, your hosiery, your black pants and skirts, your winter coats, boots and even socks. My point is to make sure you have the essentials in your wardrobe covered. The essentials are on sale too you know! Everyone restocks the basic house-hold items when they go on sale – don't forget to restock your wardrobe basics too!

Set a budget beforehand
Don't just bring a stack of plastic – that's a disaster waiting to happen. Go to the website of the stores you know you are going to shop and visit their size-chart link. Know your general sizes in those stores ahead of time so you can pull the clothing precisely. You might be a large at Ann Taylor, but you are going to be a small at Eileen Fisher! Knowledge is power and it will save you loads of frustration. If you know you are a petite for example, call ahead to see if they carry petites in that location. Some smaller stores sacrifice the petite department based on the square footage.

Pick a category to shop for

Have a basic clue what you might need to update your wardrobe and only shop for that category. How much less painful would it be if you were only shopping for shoes and handbags? Only shopping for dresses? Only shopping for a new pair of jeans? You already feel more relaxed knowing you are not going to the candle shop if you are looking for jeans and you are not going to Victoria's Secret if you are looking for shoes! Make it easy on yourself – break it down in advance.

Don't buy something with the thought that you can always return it!
You know full well you would rather have it collect dust in your closet than make another trek to the outlet mall to make a twenty dollar return.

Buy what you love, not what you like.

Plan the Mall

Don't just plan which mall, plan the floor plan of that mall! Wasted steps are wasted time and energy. Go to the mall's website. Download the map and the directory. Ever try to find the directory once inside the mall? Most malls now have volumes of additional kiosk vendors hucking games, candles, and skin lotion, but try and find the directory?!

Plan the Parking Space

Park with purpose! Maybe plan two trips to the car. Or park and then walk to the furthest destination so that all of your steps are heading back to the car. Pick your parking space based on where you plan to shop. No point parking near Yankee Candle if you hate the smell of Cranberry Pine wax. Print the mall map before you park, check off the stores you know you are going to visit and plan the parking and the exit strategy accordingly. Plan to move the car if necessary – oftentimes malls are built with anchor stores, meaning their best department stores are at opposite ends of the property. No point in slogging through the middle, if you are only shopping the anchors.

Plan the VIP Discounts

Check to see if you can sign up as a VIP on the Mall website. VIP status usually means you are signing up for their emails – you can always unsubscribe later – but be sure to take advantage of the first shot of goodies! They may include a coupon book with discounts to many stores, as well as first day specials for the new VIP! Then check out the website before you leave, as the stores post the daily and weekly deals right on the mall page offering both printable coupons as well as the option of scanning your phone once inside the store. If you don't do all of these things, you are leaving money on the table!

Plan the Price

Just because it's on sale, doesn't mean it's on sale – what? Are you really aware of the regular price? Was that high ticket item really EVER sold at that high ticket price? Be a savvy shopper. If you are really planning on shopping on Black Friday for example, then you should already know what you are looking for and what you should pay. Do your homework – do a Google search for the item itself, open the top five links, and check the price at different retailers! Your best price might be online, so why get in the car?

Plan the Savings

Shop early! Seriously Christmas decorations are in the stores in October, do you really think those deep discounts are only on Black Friday? Most stores have marked things down 48 to 72 hours before the stores even open on Friday, even if it is a 4 am opening. So shop your favorite stores online in advance.

Plan What to Wear

Dress comfortably in layers so you can quickly peel something off without always securing a dressing room. Wear comfortable shoes – this isn't a fashion show, it's a shopping expedition.

Carry a bottle of water – hydration is key to creativity.
Carry a snack such as almonds so you are not forced to buy some Fanny Farmer chocolate to avoid fainting.

Super Secret Tips

Put your items in your online shopping cart and leave them there. Monitor them daily to see if they have been marked down. If you are on the store mailing list in advance, chances are very high that they will not bump your stuff out of your cart. Just be sure to log in before shopping away. Check back on your cart often – it's kind of like playing the slot machines, every time you pull the handle the price just might change! Just be careful because they might sell out if it is that ever-so-special piece!

Some outlet stores don't advertise their discounts because they may decide the day before based on their weekly sales or what the store next door is offering, so call ahead and ask!

Price matching
You don't know if you don't ask. If it is a name brand, many department stores will price match a discount that another store is offering – again, just ask.

Be a savvy shopper
Know what designer pieces actually cost so you can spot a bargain or spot a ruse! Not all bargains are created equal – some outlet items are actually manufactured for the outlet store and therefore are the regular price 24/7!

Be smart
Use your smartphone! Unsure if it is a bargain, google it.
Don't shop when you are in a bad mood, you will overspend!
Remember plan, plan, plan, so you can shop with purpose!

"Imagine my delight when I arrived home from a grueling workday to find over twenty fabulous clothing items waiting to be tried on in the comfort of my bedroom! I poured a glass of chardonnay and jumped in. My next surprise, everything fit, looked amazing and was within my budget – big time SCORE! " DR

POWER PLAY

When it is time to step into the zone, make a powerful presence and enter the room loud and proud, your best weapon in your toolkit is your wardrobe. And here's the good news – the power suit has come a long way baby! It is definitely still a challenge to find that perfect weapon, so let's find out the new rules for power suits.

We have come a long way since Dolly Parton's "9 To 5" song. It is now okay to not look like the guys and it is encouraged to take it a step further and look fully fabulous. We understand you must dress within the parameters of your office dress code, but you must, must maintain your style and identity.

The definition of a "suit" has changed in that is does not necessarily mean matching fabrics anymore. There is of course, the menswear option for the more conservative careers such as banking, but style is being infused in the cut, the detail, the tailoring, and the trim. These women are looking to play the role, but they are playing it up by looking powerful, tailored, sophisticated, and stylish.

Then there is the suit that is not a suit by the traditional definition. It is separates, coordinated to create a cohesive outfit, balancing color, texture and proportion.

However we define the suit here, it is important to take away the notion that each piece of the "suit" should have character. The jacket, the skirt and/or the pant should have stand-alone details such as interesting patterns, fabrications, stitching, trimmings, zippers, buttons, pockets or vents. The possibilities are endless.

Let's talk jackets…no more do you have to settle for what might be the first-option-you-find, a boring black or navy single breasted, flap pocket, no vent in the back jacket. Yawn…keep shopping girlfriend.

Here is a bit of inspiration from a recent corporate client, "Here's my bottom line – I have arrived, I do not have to be one of the guys. I have the job, I have the power, I have the option and I choose to be different, express my personality, dress to the nines, and love every minute of it!"

You go girl!

First, let's talk about the essentials necessary to start to build your future style success!

Building a Working Wardrobe

A 2 or 3-piece suit – jacket, skirt & pant

Crisp, white, no-iron long sleeve shirt

Patterned or colorful long sleeve blouse

Patterned or colorful short sleeve or sleeveless blouse

Day dress

Textured jacket

Patterned separate skirt

Dark wash jeans to wear with heels

Classic or statement necklace

Classic thin belt, neutral or color

Pop of color handbag

Pop of color scarf

Nude closed toe heels

Black closed toe heels

Budgeting a Working Wardrobe

Second, let's talk money sense!

Budgeting a Working Wardrobe

A 2 or 3-piece suit – jacket, skirt & pant ($90, $60, $70)

Crisp, white, no-iron long sleeve shirt ($60)

Patterned or colorful long sleeve blouse ($50)

Patterned or colorful short sleeve or sleeveless blouse ($50)

Day dress ($90)

Textured jacket ($90)

Patterned separate skirt ($60)

Dark wash jeans to wear with heels ($60)

Classic or statement necklace ($40)

Classic thin belt, neutral or color ($20)

Pop of color scarf ($15)

Pop of color handbag ($50)

Nude closed toe heels ($50)

Black closed toe heels ($50)

Let's work the numbers so you understand.

Mind you, these are average prices; you could shop at higher or lower price points. I have reflected mid-price, better quality stores, such as Banana Republic, Lord & Taylor, Ann Taylor and the like.

The total "retail" price for this package is $905. Now before you drop your coffee, let's dive deeper. Most discounts and family-day coupons run between 25 and 30%. Let's be conservative and deduct 25% (-$226.25) – now we are down to $678.75.

Stay with me here…

Did you happen to count the number of items we have in our cart? That magic number is 16. Divide the total cost of $678.75 by 16 and your average cost per item is down to $42.42.

Are you happy so far? Here's more good news…

If you wear these items only once a week …drum roll please…your cost per wear, per item is $42.42 divided by 52 (weeks per year) = 82 CENTS!

82 cents ladies – now I call that shopping with purpose!

CLIENT STORY

Body challenges and shopping – it's like caging cats with dogs – volatile! One of my East Coast clients had her share of challenges: she was 5'4", with a size 12 petite top (very short torso) and a size 6 regular slim bottom. She needed three outfits for a West Coast conference where she was the keynote speaker. I jumped all over that challenge! We shopped at Talbots for the jackets because their jackets are a menswear cut with a deeper armhole which results in a better fit for the fuller busted woman. Her pants came from Banana Republic because their Sloan pant comes in slim and has that magic bit of Lycra. Her skirts came from Ann Taylor because she had great gams and their skirts run a bit shorter. VOILA – style challenge beat! Wait, not so fast. She arrived in her LA hotel and realized she had forgotten the entire pant category! Not an issue! Because we noted everything she purchased, right down to the SKU numbers in her digital lookbook, she contacted the Banana Republic local store and had the replacement pants delivered right to her hotel room.

Crisis diverted! Her talk was a smashing success, in case you were wondering.

The Black Story

What can't you do with an impeccably tailored tweed jacket? Let me count the ways: bring life to your black separates, pair it up with your little black dress or pop it over your fitted white T-shirt and a pair of boot cut jeans. Don't forget the bling to complete the trio of color, texture and shine.

CHAPTER 7

Are you ready for your encore?
No time like the present

It's almost a forgotten art –

Putting yourself first. You even question where to begin.

You've reached out to me for the magic makeover. You know the ones you see on Oprah and Good Morning America, where in 30 minutes they have completely transformed Dowdy Dorothy into Stunning Sophia (I even saw a whole new set of teeth popped in one morning!) But the problem with that is that when Stunning Sophia goes home and washes her face and puts on her jammies, Dowdy Dorothy is the last person she sees before closing her eyes. Pretty sure you can guess who rises from that bed in the morning.

That's why the makeover, the transformation, needs to go deeper from the start. We need to talk about the before, the daydreams, the hopes, the stumbling blocks, and the detours that turned your clothing into a less-than-stellar wardrobe that is wreaking havoc with your self-esteem and self-image. Your image becomes your excuse for why you can't embark on something new – anything new!

We just learned ladies, that the wardrobe was fixable. The stumbling block was not insurmountable. You can look fabulous at any price point. You just need to know what fits, flatters, will diligently serve you going forward into the next phase, and what to let go of!

You don't have room for something new if you never purge the old stuff! You'll never get a new hairstyle if you keep going back to the same salon. Your complexion will never look young and dewy if your makeup is old and moldy. You will never look well appointed if your favorite necklace is made of macaroni shells. And you are never going to rock that black slim skirt if you wear it with white socks and clogs

TiME TO REiNVENT YOURSELF

If you are going to embark on something new, you first have to get in touch with yourself and jumpstart your self-confidence.

Maybe you've sent a child off to college, or a dear friend to a new job in a new city, and no doubt you said, "You can do it – I believe in you". Well now it's your turn – you can do it, you need to believe in you. And if it takes some steps to get you there, then put yourself on your own to-do list and take those steps. But in order to get your engine revved up – you need to take care of your self-esteem and that starts with how you feel about your own image.

When you see yourself in the mirror are you looking at who you were or who you want to be? Embrace this time as a wonderful opportunity to get to know you. Start your "ME" to do list and pinpoint what you need to outsource. This is a wonderful time to discover new confidence and well being. And by all means if you are looking for something deeper than a magic makeover, give me a call. We'll share a cup of coffee in the shadow of your closet! www.DoreenDove.com/contact

Hair, there, everywhere

Look for a NEW hairdresser! Come on ladies – unless there is a marriage certificate between you, no one has to stay with the same hairdresser for a lifetime! As bored as you are with the same old, same old, they too are most likely bored with you! It is a vicious cycle – they don't want to change it up for fear you won't embrace a change and then you might wander...over to the dark side (the shop across the street). At the same time they are looking at their schedule book and saying (don't fool yourself, they are saying this out loud), "Oh Betty is coming in today – ho hum, same old, same old!" Take the bull by the horns and take control of your own destiny! Take a chance – this isn't a trip to the moon Alice! Your hair actually grows back and there are many colors in the Crayola box so if you don't like a color, you just pick another one.

The Skin of It

News flash - as you age your skin tone changes so you need to adjust the border and the paint – the hair and the makeup! Otherwise the mismatch makes you look older than you are.

We've come a long way baby. There are night creams, day creams, eye creams, waxing creams, dyeing creams and on and on. The point here is you should be using "creams" as early as your teens to keep your skin soft and supple.

Then there is the magic makeup. Similar to what I said above about changing it up with your hair..change up your makeup. Old mascara, mineral powders and eye shadow can actually grow bacteria. Oooh, that sounds delightful. Splurge and outsource your makeup. There is no shortage of companies and types of makeup. Take the time to check out some options. Start paying attention to beauty magazines, take a stroll through the makeup counters or check out makeup artists from your local spas. Just give it a try – let someone else paint your palette so you can pick up ideas. The way you apply might be totally wrong. For example did you know that your eyes look smaller when you use an eyeliner under your eyes? It is now recommended to use a liner as an edge on your upper eyelashes and only pop mascara on the bottom, thereby opening up your eyes! Let an expert have a go at your face, you are bound to be amazed what a different product, in a different color, applied in a different manner can do for your mug!

Show stopping legs

When you get out of the shower tomorrow – look at your legs. No really – get up close and personal with them!

Step #1 Can you spell exfoliate? Oh, must I remove that dead skin – it's the only thing left of my vacation tan from six months ago! Eeeew – yes – it must go! Before you lather up to shave your legs, give them an exfoliating scrub down. Exfoliation sloughs off the dry, flaky skin that can prevent a close shave and it brings the hairs to the surface so that they're easier to remove. There is no shortage of natural "food" choices to do the sloughing. Pick an abrasive body scrub with ingredients such as salt, sugar, or oatmeal. A scrub and a shave and you'll be homefree, trotting out your sleek, baby soft gams in no time.

Step # 2 De-fuzzing
De-fuzzing – also known as shaving. Unless you have lasered your worries away – a good shave is a requirement. Go buy a new "lady" razor. My favorite – Gillette Venus – 5 blades and a touch of Aloe for sensitive skin! You can also find swiveling ball hinges and battery operated doo-dahs, so what's not to like? But will it make your legs look like silk or just feel like silk? All kidding aside…ya gotta de-pill to get anywhere near smooth. After exfoliating, shaving and showering, towel off all product and wait ten minutes until you are 100 percent dry.

the skin of it...

Now you are ready to get tanning! This advice is critical – choose a self-tanner for your skin tone, not your desired result! Nobody gets a Coppertone tan with just one day on the beach! Make this a gradual process and the outcome will be close to perfection. Rush the project, and a "Jersey Shore" look may be the result!

Let's talk product – mousses and lotions are easiest to rub in and sprays can sometimes end up not where intended. Start with each calf area and gradually stretch the lotion to the ankles and feet, applying less on the foot area. Do both calves then do both thighs, gradually stretching that product to the knees. Remember to bend your knees so you do not miss getting product in the creases (yes, we all have creases). Now go scrub your hands if you weren't wearing plastic painter's gloves when you applied the lotion. Be patient, if it says dry for 10 minutes, wait 20. You can apply a talc-free powder on your legs to stop the tanner from staining your clothing or your sheets. Do not sweat or shower for 8 hours.

Ooooh, big vacation coming up? The secret to smart packing is PLANNING. Let's start planning by distinguishing what you want to bring from what you need to bring. Oftentimes we are forced to choose from our favorite things, so we bring all of them. Bad idea.

Let's move through the top ten tips (and talk you down from the cliff) to get you mentally and physically prepared.

Do your homework – check the extended weather forecast, check out venues for your events, check last year's conference photos so you know how attendees were dressed, if it is a hosted event like a wedding, check in with the host.

Do an at home reality check, if you wear your jeans or black dress pants an average of 3 times a week at home, don't pack 3 pair of jeans and 3 pair of black pants for a 3-day trip.

Create a wardrobe plan for each day of your trip, morning, noon, and night. Write it down and then make it visual. Pull the outfits out and lay them on the bed, or even better, on a small collapsible garment rack. Whenever anyone is packing in my home, the garment rack appears about a week before so we can accumulate the items as we think about them, or as they come home from the dry cleaners or emerge from the laundry room.

Scrutinize each item. Do you ever wear it at home? Does having that 20-pound sweater justify carrying that 20-pound sweater in your suitcase?

Don't pack for the worst-case scenario – pack for the best-case scenario. Why lug a raincoat in case it rains? Bring layers of clothing instead (plus where have you ever gone that they don't sell umbrellas?)

When in doubt, leave it out. If you really don't like it on the bed, you're not going to like it on your bod!

Take a reality pill. Pack the same for 2-weeks as you would for 1 week. You are not going to lug 14 days worth of clothing around the country with you. Can you spell LAUNDROMAT? When stuck in LA for an extra 6 days on a recent trip, I had to do laundry, and yes I had to search on the outskirts of town because there weren't any in Beverly Hills (shocker), but I survived on what I had packed for the first 5 days.

Stretch your outfits with accessories! One solid blouse or dress can be dressed up or down with different jewels or shoes. You do it at home, do it on the road.

Pack only garments that can be color coordinated with everything else in your suitcase – think capsules! If there is only one red item in the batch and it requires red shoes that can only be worn with that outfit, get rid of the red!

If packing for a 7-day trip, take note of everything you wear the week before. You'll be surprised at how few things you made it through the week with and how many times you repeated the same items.

Last tips:
If you can't imagine your life without the crown jewels, then don't risk losing them on a trip – lock them up at home.

Don't bring every gadget you own – seriously how much repetitive info can you look at on your iPhone, your iPad, your Kindle and your laptop? To say nothing of all the plugs that they require!

Don't pack things you can buy there or use there. Most hotels have good-enough toiletries, hair dryers, sewing kits, etc.

Bag check – what's in my suitcase you ask?

- 1 pair of boyfriend jeans
- 1 dark wash dressier skinny jean
- 1 black ankle length straight leg trouser
- 1 Lululemon crop pant for exercising, walking in the desert
- 1 pair of shorts – for lounging around the hotel
- 2 dressy T's – one white, one graphic
- 2 tank liners, one white, and one black
- 1 sweater
- 1 stylish loose jacket
- 1 sleep shirt
- Undies, bras – one white, nude and black
- 2 rockin' blouses, one sleeveless, one long sleeve
- 2 rockin' necklaces and some stacking bracelets
- 1 dress for the special event – long sleeve so no layering piece necessary
- 1 flat sandal – for jeans
- 1 heeled sandal – for dress pant
- 1 strappy shoe for the dress

Recap

The outfits: 3 pants, 2 T's, 1 sweater, 2 blouses, 1 jacket, and 1 dress
The lounging and undies: 2 bottoms, 2 tank liners, 1 sleep shirt, and undies.
The peripherals: 3 shoes, 2 necklaces, and a few bracelets
Toiletries

Special Occasion Dressing

The holiday season is a whirlwind of errands – shopping, wrapping, cleaning, baking, decorating, and driving! And plenty of excuses to dress up and party! Yikes, do YOU not end up on your own shopping list? Are you spending half the holidays fretting about how to muster up enough energy to throw open your closet doors and pull together something fabulous for those office Christmas parties, Hannukah bashes, and the New Year's Eve soiree? Here's the bottom line. If you have some of these key items in your closet, consider yourself good to go. If not, then perhaps in the midst of returning all those unwanted sweaters, you can pick up a few party savers for yourself.

The Little Black Dress – Let's state the obvious first and get it over with. Most every woman has that great LBD, one that accentuates your body (where it deserves accentuating) and forgives and conceals those areas that need it. Have some fun with old faithful for the holidays, add a belt in exotic faux skin, paired with high black boots, or play off your gorgeous gams with a sexy (and oh so appropriate) red heel. Your jewelry can be a simple bold cuff or a statement necklace.

The Metallic Evening Shoe – When darting from the office to a post-work holiday gathering, simply switching up your sensible black pumps to a flirty pair of metallic shoes will turn your basic black pantsuit or demure black pencil skirt, into a glam statement of confidence. Your options are endless – strappy sandals, kitten heels, sequined adorned, ballet flats and more, it all reads more festive in silver or gold.

The Sequined Tank – Nothing says "Happy New Year" quite like sequins. (OK maybe champagne does…) The beauty of a sequined tank is that it flatters women of most any shape and age. Pair it with skinny jeans and heels, a pair of dark, tailored men's trousers or a skirt. Cropped jackets, trenches, tuxedo-style blazers and denim jackets all work to downplay the arms (if needed) and keep you warm.

The Black Story

The dressy black jacket is a must in every wardrobe. It is your go to for finishing off the evening dress, pairing up with a sassy slim skirt (think eggplant leather) or rock it with a pair of skinny jeans and a sexy pump. I have chosen this single breasted, one button with a leather collar and finished off with a pleated back because as I always say – you have to look good when you leave the room!

special occasion dressing...

Statement Jewelry – Make it bold and make it yours. A string of pearls, although always a classic, does not a strong impression make. Take any outfit (jeans and a T?) and give it instant party cred by donning a big, boldly cut, chunky cocktail ring. Festive emerald in celebration of the season perhaps? The epic chandelier earring, with gemstones or faux jewels could also do the trick.

Leather – Leather has for years been a go-to holiday staple in my own closet. Pair up some butter-soft black leather pants with a cashmere sweater and high heels for a party look that is almost as comfortable as pajama bottoms. A leather pencil skirt with a fabulous blouse, opaque tights, and heels can also be a reliable staple. One of the best things about leather – you won't have to waste time ironing!

White Blouse – For holidays it should be anything BUT the basic work button down. Try something with ruffles, tuxedo style, big cuffs, taffeta, sheer, halter... the options are endless! Choose a style that complements your figure, then pair it with skinny or trouser jeans, menswear pants, black skirts, leather pants, even ball gown skirts!

Evening Clutch – Leave the oversized hobo bag at work. For holiday parties, keep your must carry essentials to a minimum (lipstick, debit card, breath mints) so they can fit in this undersized accessory. Let the statement come from its art and craftsmanship, and choose jewel encrusted or slim and trimmed in satin. For once, bigger is not necessarily better.

Fashionably fun leg coverings – I'm hesitant to use the term "hose" lest it conjure up images of nurses in their white panty hose and my own nightmare memories of baggy elephant legs after my sheer nylons lost their stretch. Today's options are much more fashion forward, even while being flashbacks in their own right. Fishnets in either black, monochromatic or flesh tone will add instant sex appeal to any dress or skirt. Opaque tights in black or unexpected bold colors will keep the winter chill off of your legs while acting as a punctuation mark to your outfit.

Red – It is the holidays after all, so celebrate with one of its hallmark colors. Bold red lips make an entrance (but be sure to balance it with a subtle eye). If you can't pull off the red lips, then opt for candy apple red nail polish. Break up your black ensemble with a red belt or scarf. However you decide to incorporate the shade of the season, remember, a small dose goes a long way.

Modern Evening Wrap – And by modern I mean, "not a shawl." Your wrap could have sleeves built in, be a shrug or sheer jacket. Ideally, it is something so unique that it stands on its own while complementing your look. One made of silk, in brighter colors with metallic threads adds a festive note. Take off the black work blazer, replace it with an unexpected topper and you will keep yourself warm while turning heads. If you have any of the above pieces already in your closet, you are ready to rock the holiday parties effortlessly. If you are lacking these evening basics, just remember while dashing to the mall to make returns, you deserve a little something special and sparkly!

> "People will stare. Make it worth their while."
> *Harry Winston*

"Imagine living where your only shopping options are WalMart – mind you that's not bad for your everyday 'stuff', but when it came to styling my image for my new business launch – that was a problem! I found myself lost, frustrated and clueless where to turn for help. I knew I need a makeover and I also knew there was no one up here in Nova Scotia to turn to. Then I found Doreen Dove online! Problem solved! She made me feel so comfortable from the first phone call and all the way through the whole process! We Skyped, chatted on the phone, exchanged photos, measurements and challenges right down to the types of shoes I needed to wear. I looked forward to each session with invigorated energy and improving self-esteem. I have to say the items that she located for me online were spot on, not one return – now that's amazing! I highly recommend Doreen to get you in shape – I have renewed confidence and am flying in my new venture! Outsource your style to Doreen –you'll love the way you look!" KB

MY LAST 2 CENTS

The secret to great fitting jeans is 5% lycra.

Downsize your clothing numbers by forcing yourself to wear something from the back of the clost - TODAY.

Dress too tight? Go green - eliminate dairy and grains for five days.

Bunions? Stick a few golf balls in your shoes, spritz with a bit of water and let them sit overnight.

New shoes too tight - fill two freezer bags with water, place them in the shoes and then place the shoes in the freezer - just be sure your stiletto doesn't pierce the cookie dough ice cream.

Panty lines are never in style - invest in Spanx or the like.

Your salad spinner is perfect for removing excess water from hand washables - who knew!

White wine removes red wine stains…on your clothes, not sure about your teeth! Work a try though…

Wash your jeans before tailoring. Wash dark wash jeans before wearing your Cole Haan cross-body…ink is the enemy.

Remove annoying white deodorant marks with those even more annoying foam covers from hangers.

Old coat too out of style? Shorten it to a jacket.

Have a few too many boring shirts in your wardrobe – snap clip-on earrings onto the collars.

Always dry clean winter items before storing them – moths love dirty clothes!

Never ever keep the cardboard shoeboxes – the only thing they are good for is dust bunnies. Your shoes should be "seen & worn".

Bra fitting – yes it's time!

Windex – oh we could go on forever, but for now it shines up those patent leather shoes just fine!

Oily skin might be coming from your hair…coming from your pillowcase!!! Change your pillowcase every two days.

Want your clothing to look more appealing – buy all new skinny black hangers.

Hoping something goes on sale – sign up for email notifications from your favorite store and plop those things in your shopping cart. Check your cart every few days.

Bored with your grocery store – reverse your aisle order! This is true for your favorite department store as well – enter from a different door, start upstairs instead of downstairs – you'll be amazed at all of the new things that catch your eye!

I hope you enjoyed this journey ladies, I encourage you to keep on it – keep reading my blog, checking out fashion magazines, noticing store displays, and just plain paying attention to what you are attracted to. This process was all about creating a new you, not just cleaning the closet out. This was a great start. If you feel you want to dive deeper and are not located on the East Coast, join the growing number of women who are virtually outsourcing their style. Updating your image and wardrobe and finding your authentic style is a very personal journey and you shouldn't be limited to your local resources. That goes for both stylists and stores!

My virtual styling package will help you define your authentic style and boost your self-confidence, getting you ready for what your future may hold. I want you to feel good, look good, and be empowered with the knowledge of how to achieve and maintain your newfound style. However, please realize that once a client, always a client. I will remain your "stylist on call", so I encourage you to keep the communication going long after we finish our sessions! www.DoreenDove.com

"Start where you are, use what you have and do what you can."
Arthur Ashe

You are ready to style it up now, you have the tools in your closet - go ahead and build something beautiful.

And remember, **Confidence Is Always In Style**

I leave you with a client's personal 'share'...

"I feel so much more confident and continue to get a ton of compliments on a daily basis. I think the best thing about the whole experience of the closet edit, shopping trip, new haircut and makeup, is that it just "stuck" for me. I am a perfect spokesperson for the value of this experience because this self-care is so far removed from my typical lifestyle. For me to fully embrace new ideas about how I present myself is a huge transformation, both psychologically as well as physically. Speaking of physically, I've already lost three pounds and feel much more motivated because I feel like I look amazing in the process! Last night, another mom asked me what my secret was for "looking so good," and I glibly replied, "Divorce."But in reality, the secret was you. You helped me to jumpstart a new me! Thank you Doreen, thank you, thank you!" LV

Remember, you are pretty

About Doreen

Doreen Dove is a highly qualified image consultant, personal stylist, speaker and author whose extensive background in all aspects of retail has uniquely qualified her to work with clients of all ages and professions, coaching them to personal style success.

As an award-winning expert in the field of Image Consulting, Doreen Dove coaches women to use style as a tool to take strategic control of their image and fully engage in the possibilities of their future.

In addition to her one-on-one work with individual clients, Doreen conducts workshops and seminars for corporate groups and speaks at conferences across the country.

Doreen's curated services include:

Complimentary Consultation: Identify your style and strategize your image breakthrough
Closet Edit: Assess your wardrobe and address what's needed
Shopping Services: Doreen shops with you or for you as you learn what to buy, where to shop and what to pay
Digital Look-Book: Never struggle again with creating your signature style with your personal go-to guide
Virtual Styling: A personalized program including phone calls, skype sessions, photo exchanges and link sharing

www.doreendove.com
doreen@doreendove.com

"You can have anything you want if you dress for it."
Edith Head

Acknowledgements

The book was accomplished using the talents of many people.

Thank you to Janice Gallardo Walters of Gallardo Graphics in Los Angeles for a beautiful layout and the access to your on-point design expertise.

Thank you to my lifelong girlfriend Beth Bullinger for creating my stunning signature line and providing her daily inspiration.

Thank you to Courtney Trembler of Soul Focus Photography for helping me illustrate my fashion vision with her beautiful photos.

Thank you to Michelle Israel Bistany and her fabulous store Recess Boutique for keeping me well dressed!

Thank you for the help of Bibi Goldstein's team at Buying Time LLC.

"Life is challenging, but we have to get dressed."
Doreen Dove

INTRODUCTION

Imagine with me for a moment...

You just got the opportunity of a lifetime.
This is the opportunity you have been waiting for.

Maybe you…

• Are launching a new business
• Are re-launching a career that has been on hold
• Are reaching for a higher position within your company
• Have the opportunity to land a million dollar client
• Are ready to start mentoring others
• Or are simply ready for the next chapter of your life

The only thing you need to do is meet with key individuals that can determine if this opportunity becomes a reality. On the day you are scheduled to meet with those decision makers, you feel confident and well dressed, despite having struggled with your closet, your clothing choices, your hair, your makeup, your shoes and even your bag that will carry your bravery. The meeting goes as planned. And then nothing. No return phone calls. No emails. You find out weeks later that they didn't choose you because they said you didn't project the right image. You are stunned that your image is negatively impacting the outcome of your dreams. It was like the opportunity you were waiting for literally got blown away.

May I share with you why I am so passionate about helping you?

I grew up in Rhode Island, a small state, in a small town, in a small house with a small family. Both my parents worked and they worked hard. As a result I was pretty independent as a kid, even coming home in elementary school to an empty house for lunch. I was pretty self-confident with the exception of my body image - I was as skinny as skinny gets and was teased relentlessly in elementary school. Coming home and eating lunch alone was a bit of a blessing. Middle school brought the big yellow bus and confined exposure to the mean girls. My rock bottom moment was when the big bully (and she was big compared to me) seized the perfect opportunity to publicly humiliate me as I got off the bus.

She bellowed out the window, "Hobble on home peg-leg." I wanted to melt into the street – nowhere to hide. It was the longest walk home ever. And as I already mentioned, I had working parents so I came home to an empty house and stuck my nose into my tattered stack of fashion magazines where my "friends" were all skinny...

One of them was Twiggy. Funny that was the only name the bully didn't call me! That day was a turning point for me and that very evening I simply asked my mother if I could be a model. The next week I found myself in the Sears Charm School learning how to cross my skinny legs when I sat down. One of my very first modeling jobs was at 15 years old standing in the window at Ann Taylor. I had arrived in a comfortable place where I could embrace my body and start to work on my self-confidence.

I share my story in an effort to show you why I am so passionate about helping you, because I am pretty sure that most of us have a story about being made to feel less than we actually are. At some point in your life there may have been a time when you were defined by someone else.

Doreen, age 15,
modeling at Ann Taylor

The minute I made the mental shift from thinking about my body as a liability to thinking about it as an asset, I was on my way – on my own path. And I have never looked back. I actually saw that perpetrator at a class reunion about 30 years later, and I have to say, I was pretty proud of peg-leg!

And now here I am decades later, writing *Confidence Is Always In Style*.

Why should you care about your image? The way you present yourself has a profound impact on your relationships and your career. The old adage, "You can't judge a book by its cover," really only applies to books because unfortunately you are judged by your cover, your appearance, your personal hygiene, your wardrobe, your costume.

Life is sometimes like a Broadway play. When that curtain opens on stage and the actor appears, you immediately form an opinion of her based on her wardrobe or her costume. You don't have the option of stripping her down to see how fabulous she is as a person. You formed your judgment immediately within 20 seconds.

If you're a professional, every second counts, from the interview to the daily job, the networking, the meetings, and the potential for advancement. Many entrepreneurs who are building a business through networking know how important every component of branding is, right down to your LinkedIn profile picture and your business cards. That first impression lasts forever.

Think about what it's costing you not to make a change. Are you not going to be attracting the right partner, the perfect clients? Are you being overlooked for promotions? Do you want to launch a new business? What does your overall package look like?

Perhaps you have a messy closet full of clothes and nothing to wear because what's in there was from a different play, a play that's outdated, maybe out of style, the wrong size, maybe even the wrong character. You don't know where to begin, what to toss, what to save, what to tailor, what to replace, where to go to replace it, what to replace it with, when to shop for it, and at what price point. Making a change will be challenging if you're not equipped with any of the answers to these questions. Many women give up even before trying.

You may be feeling a sudden sense of "I'm overwhelmed." You shut the closet door. You've got a meeting that you have to get dressed for. Your black pants are at the dry cleaner again. It's drama and it's a waste of time.

We've got to get you in the right place to not only clean out your closet, but eliminate the unnecessary stress! Let's get to work on 'you' empowering you. This book will teach you how to get to know your body, like your body, dress your body and become your biggest fan!

Remember -
CONFIDENCE
is always in style

Know your body: No two women are built alike and that is what makes us special. Become familiar with your body type, as knowledge is power. Are you average, petite or tall? Where do you carry your weight - fuller on the top, fuller on the bottom, or fuller in the middle? We all carry it somewhere. Let's define it where you are today, not 10 pounds in the past or future, and move forward with purpose.

Like your body: I have always chuckled at the saying, "I am in shape: round is a shape!" It pretty much sums up the fact that we as women come in all shapes and sizes and each one comes with styling challenges. We are who we are, so let's just embrace our genetics and work with what we have. Clothing can become our ally when we want to highlight our assets or conceal our less favorable features – that's called "styling!"

Dress your body: The first step towards transformation is to stop thinking something is wrong with your body and start recognizing something is wrong with your clothes. By learning how to choose clothing that properly fits your shape and highlights your assets, you will discover your style. Your wardrobe will be well thought out, your closet will become a happy place, and the art of shopping will become joyful once again.

Once you conquer the understanding of fit and proportion, your confidence will soar. By embracing the principles of style you will be ready to discover how color, accessories, and fashion details can be used to accentuate your best features and help you to strike the perfect balance of style and sophistication, with the ultimate goal being a well-balanced wardrobe that is time-efficient and flattering every single day, no matter what you reach in and pull out.

It is my goal with this book to empower women to thrive in their self-confidence and to achieve all that is possible. I share my thoughts, suggestions, and expertise with a bit of honey (humor) as it always helps the medicine (tough love) go down!

Enjoy!

Doreen

CHAPTER 1

Clueless About Your Style?
Welcome to the masses!

The first step towards transformation is for you to
stop thinking something is wrong with your body
and realize there is something wrong with your clothing!

While it may look like a purely creative endeavor, there is a science to style. Together we can crack the code!

Let start by gathering some facts as they relate to you. Are you average, petite or tall? Identify where you carry your weight, as we all carry it somewhere. Define it and then move forward and be able to shop with purpose.

Knowledge is power!

No longer is it necessary to slog around the mall trying to find something that fits, flatters, and is within your budget. If you just walk in the mall not knowing in advance what you're looking for then you won't accomplish the ultimate goal, which is a well-balanced wardrobe that is time-efficient and flattering every single day.

KNOW YOUR STYLE

Have you seen the annual 20-pound edition of Vogue magazine that comes out each season? It's known as the "fashion bible" in some circles! If you think a fashion magazine is not for you…think again. Grab a Vogue, InStyle, More, Lucky, Elle, or Marie Claire and let's go!

Follow my protocol…pour a glass of wine, grab a stack of sticky notes and a pen or marker (any stylish color will do) and settle into a quiet space for "me" time.

"We engaged Doreen to help our daughter to update her image and shop with her to fill her wardrobing needs. Doreen is incredibly knowledgeable as an image consultant and quite personable and was able to relate with our daughter and help her to fill those needs easily and with fun! We plan to continue working with her in the future." JW

know your style...

Now go page by page, and find something you "like" on each page. Use a sticky note and record what you like about it. Forget the price, and forget that the model is a twig, and just stay with me here.

The following types of things can be noted...love that merlot color, that two-tone shoe, that tweed coat, that statement necklace, that jacket collar, those fancy bronze buttons, the textured heel on that boot, the color of that nail polish, the style of that skirt, the yarn of that sweater, those high waist pants, that colorblock handbag and on and on! This becomes a mental exercise for you to get out of the repeat zone. The repeat zone is defined as buying the same thing over and over again, which is boring even for you!

Not sure you are a repeat offender? Do you take the same path through the grocery store every week and pick up the same things? Try reversing your order next week, going down the "up" aisle and watch how many new things magically appear in your cart! Shopping for clothing is the same process. If you always go to the same store and follow the same path within the store, you will leave with the same looks that you have been wearing for - well - maybe decades!

Has your taste in food, music, movies, or men changed over the years? Well keep up girlfriend, so should your style. Fashion is supposed to be fun, expressive, and current. Is your style fun, expressive, and current? If not, time to pay attention. Pay attention to what you ask? For starters notice what is being worn on television, in the movies, in the store windows, and in the magazines! Simply, start paying attention!

Time to try something new. Let's tweak your thought process. Some clients even rip out the pages and throw them in a folder so that when they go shopping they can be inspired to go into a different store, reverse their order in their favorite department store, or even venture into local boutiques! Now pour the wine, grab the sticky notes and get to work!

Take a look at these two magazines after they have been worked over by two clients. There are tabs on all sides, noting all things that they found appealing and even some that they didn't. The point is they felt comfortable to be the judge, jury and the designer of their future shopping trips. They now have ideas, visions, plans, and lists so they can shop with purpose! Once you have a game plan, you can even shop online in advance.

Try this exercise. Say your favorite store is Nordstrom and after playing the sticky note game you have decided that this season a tweed jacket is to your liking. Go to www.Nordstrom.com and type "womens tweed jacket" in the search box. See what I mean? Look at the options that you can find that you might not have even walked by in the store. You can check the fabric, the size scale, the price, and my favorite—the actual availability in your local store! How you ask? Online chat – rev that up and tell them the style number, the size and the zip-code of your local store – they will tell you if it is on the sales floor. Then you could even call ahead and have the store hold it for you in advance. Come on ladies, short of having me shop with you (which of course is the best option), could I possibly make this any easier for you?

COLOR, TEXTURE & SHINE

I first became familiar with the phrase "color, texture, and shine" a few years back while working with Stacy London of the television show *What Not To Wear.* As she shared her fashion expertise with us, she always spoke in terms of color, texture, and shine, almost insisting that a client had to have the daily requirement of those three components before she walked out the door. She encouraged us to use the rule, teach the rule, and live personally by the rule. I have to say, I am a fan and make sure before I walk out my own door that I have filled in the blanks on all three fronts.

COLOR

The use of color in your daily garb not only flatters your overall appearance, but it can influence your mood as well as the mood of others around you. The first thing that people notice about you is the color you are wearing! As all of us black lovers know, the power of the color black can instantly erase 10 pounds! The power of a "real" color can erase about 10 years from your look by complementing your hair and skin tone.

color...

The first step is to ascertain the color palette that suits your skin tone best. Skin tones are categorized by the seasons - spring, summer, autumn and winter. The season you belong to is in turn determined by the tone and contrast of your skin. If you have a "warm" tone, your skin has deeper undertones of gold and yellow with visible veins appearing green-ish. A "cool" tone means your skin is pale with pink or blue undertones and the veins will normally look blue-ish. Then determine whether your contrast is high or low (the difference between your skin tone and your hair color).

Warm and high = Spring   Warm and low = Autumn
Cool and high = Winter   Cool and low = Summer

Pick up a color wheel at any art supply or craft store as it can help you figure out which colors in your wardrobe can be mixed and matched. First, simply look at colors that are opposite on the color wheel – for example, purple and yellow, or blue and orange. These opposite colors work very well together because they contrast each other. Secondly, notice how red and purple, situated next to each other on the color wheel, look great together because they compliment each other. The two "C" words contrast and complement – use them to your advantage. The third way to use the color wheel is to dress in one color, but in different hues. Using several shades of the same color, from light to dark, will give you a polished look.

Color is the most important component of your look and it's the easiest way to freshen your wardrobe and reflect your own personal style. Remember that color can be pulled into your look with fabrics, accessories, shoes, and even your lipstick or nail polish.

TEXTURE

Texture gives your outfit depth and interest. The texture could be the weave of the fabric, the density of the cloth, the "skin" of the belt or even the composition of the necklace. When working with clients, I often use texture to either accentuate the assets or disguise the liabilities. Here's one example for both categories. Say your body proportion is fuller on the bottom and we need to balance out your silhouette by adding a bit of volume to the top of your frame. The best way to do that is by using a textured jacket or a blouse, something tweedy, nubby and perhaps colorful. Or we would add color or shine with the accessories (scarves, necklaces, etc.) to bring the eye away from the fuller-on-the-bottom liability up to your beautiful face and neckline, accentuating the assets.

SHINE

Shine could be your glossy lipstick, your patent leather shoe, your silky shimmery blouse, and of course, your bling! Let's talk bling specifically, as most women love jewels! I personally do not leave the house without my 4-point jewelry checklist – earrings, watch, multiple bracelets and a necklace.

I wish I could say that I vary my earrings, but admittedly I am lazy and love my diamonds. My

watches are a choice of two, one dressy and one a bit sportier with a leather band. My necklaces and bracelets are where I really express myself. I have been a bit of a collector over time making sure I have the demure and chunky gold, as well as the demure and chunky silver. I have pearls but never wear them; somehow I wore them more in my twenties when we were wearing those obligatory menswear suits and floppy bow ties! Oh my, how far we have come!

Perhaps my packing the pearls away was a bit more ceremonial than I realized! These days I opt for statement pieces because I love variety, and what better way to change up an outfit than with your necklace – there it is, front and center, begging for attention!

It's not rocket science ladies; it's just the creative process. Build your wardrobe and build your outfit before you walk out the door! Remember, fashion is supposed to be FUN! However if you are struggling then perhaps it is time to outsource your style!

CLIENT STORY

I received a voicemail from a young woman who simply said, "My name is Jennifer and on a scale of 1-10, my sense of style is a zero. I am clueless where to even begin and I start a new job in the finance sector in 4 days!" During the consult call she shared that she was always an athlete, was raised in a house of boys, never learned how to style her athletic body, how to shop, or what to shop for, and had never bought a dress or worn heels. We started by finding a great fitting pair of pants, as that is the hardest item of clothing to fit. With her athletic thighs we searched out "curvy" fits by store, but we made sure those stores also had the matching jackets as an option because the dress code was suits. We had to accommodate her muscular thighs first and foremost (you have to fit for the largest measurement and then tailor down). The tailor took in the waist less than one inch and hemmed them to perfection. We moved on to the jacket, searching for a cut that was fuller through the shoulders. The tailor nipped in the waist and shortened the sleeves so it looked like it was custom made. The shoes were tricky as she had never worn heels and was going to be a city commuter. The last thing I was going to do was put her in a pair of wobbly heels which would make her even more nervous on her first day at the office. So we opted for a black one-inch wedge with a pointed toe embellished with grosgrain and patent leather. We shopped for a necklace and a tote bag and she was done. I say "done" because she was now empowered with the knowledge of what looked good on her, where she should shop for her clothing, what price she should pay, and what tailoring she should expect based on her body profile. She was well equipped with the know-how for all of her future shopping trips!

For the Love of Black:

The Black Story

Just stating the facts here – your wardrobe is dysfunctional without the black foundational building blocks. I often tell my clients one of the most important pieces in their wardrobe is a traffic-stopping great fitting pair of black pants.

Come on ladies, I know you can relate. They are your go-to item to make you feel skinny, confident and oh yes, well-dressed. This isn't rocket science – black is easy! Match those pants up with a well-fitting, sassy shell and you have the foundation for a limitless number of outfits from the clothing that already exists in your closet!

Here I am in my black foundational pieces. As you work your way through this book, keep your eyes peeled for a few of the outfits that I built around this foundation!

You'll see simple additions such as necklaces, jackets, or blouses. Don't over complicate this, ladies – keep it simple, enjoy the process, and embrace the outcome!

What every well-dressed woman should own; a well tailored pair of black pants. When you find them, buy two pair and hem one for flats and one for heels. You will also need a few black fine quality shells. I recommend one crew neck and one v-neck with wide enough shoulders to not expose any bra straps – ever. Finish it off with fashionable black footwear. I recommend owning flats, pumps and booties for variety.

CHAPTER 2

What Shape Am I?
Round, round is a shape!

One of the biggest mistakes women make when dressing their bodies is not understanding their specific body type. Show your body some respect! Quite honestly, where to shop, what to buy, and what to pay are all valid questions, but before you can tackle those you must answer the dreaded question, "What shape am I?"

A common answer is, "Round – round is a shape!" Many women have been brainwashed into thinking they must answer with a cute and non-offensive elementary school term such as "pear" or "apple". Then there are those math types who need everything to have quadrants – I am a "rectangle", "triangle" or even an "inverted" triangle.

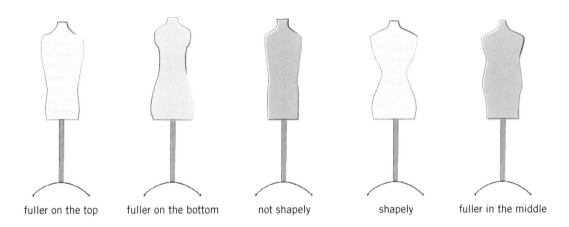

| fuller on the top | fuller on the bottom | not shapely | shapely | fuller in the middle |

I will never use a fruit to describe your body type! Let's just state the facts, Watson. While we are doing that, let's really define "average".

According to the Centers for Disease Control*, the average sizes for women in the US are as follows:

Height (inches): 63.8
Weight (pounds): 166.2
Waist circumference (inches): 37.5

This means the average woman is about 5'4", weighs 166 pounds, and probably is wearing a size 18 or so. Were you expecting something different? Perhaps something like the 5'8" and 120 pound size that we see in all the magazines? Relax, we knew that just wasn't realistic anyway.
We all carry our weight somewhere. No need to panic! Let's determine what body type is the best fit for you (pun intended). Then read on for style suggestions so you can rock the body you have – today!

* http://www.cdc.gov/nchs/fastats/body-measurements.htm

Here are the basic body terms I use with my clients:

Fuller on the top: Simply put, your bust measurement
is fuller than your hips and rear.

Fuller on the bottom: You are fuller at the hips and
rear and smaller on the top.

Fuller in the middle: There is a little extra in the middle
resulting in your narrowest measurement being just above
the natural waist at the ribs.

Shapely: You are a curvy girl with a full bust, a defined waist
and full hips resulting in the ultimate hourglass figure.

Not Shapely: There is very little difference between your bust,
waist and hip measurement.

You generally know what looks best on you – perhaps there's a wrap dress that
consistently makes you feel confident or you always gravitate toward wide-leg
pants – but I figured a more in-depth look at dressing for your body type is
never a bad idea. Keep reading to find your body type and my tips to maximize
the assets and disguise the liabilities.

FULLER ON THE TOP

If you're fuller on the top, I find the biggest mistake that women make is to shop at stores that specialize in draping - we all know what stores those are so I won't call them out. If you are shopping there, your whole style might be built around draping loose fabrics in the attempt to hide - also know as tenting!

Here's the bad news: you're only creating a more obvious imbalance, making you appear even larger on the top and smaller on the bottom. We call that the light bulb silhouette!

What we're going for is the hourglass silhouette, which is big, small, big. A great way to accomplish this silhouette with a fuller on the top proportion is to look for solid color jackets with a bit of structure in the tailoring to define the waistline. Then coordinate with a patterned blouse to create a vertical line down the front. Finish the outfit off with an A-line skirt to complete the hourglass effect. A classic v-neck wrap dress in a rich fabric also draws the eye up and down for a slimming effect. And of course, a great support bra is a must! More on that later.

Try to steer clear of the skinny-style pants, which will over-accentuate your larger top and create an imbalanced look. Look for a bootcut trouser, with a little bit of a flare to balance the width of the shoulders or bust for that big, small, big hourglass look.

TAILORING TIP: Tailor your trousers on the longer side. Ask for a break in the front, thereby angling the hemline length towards the back. This will elongate the look of the legs.

Client Story

I recently was shopping with a client who lost close to 100 pounds. Despite this epic accomplishment, she still was withholding personal permission to look and feel sassy. She was still wearing clothing one full size larger than her current frame. By trying on smaller sizes and having the conversation about self-confidence, she came to realize that she indeed looked fabulous. She left with new clothing, in the right size, and a newfound respect for the new woman that she now is!

We're going to do the reverse if you are fuller on the bottom and slimmer on the top. You want to add volume on the top, by incorporating color, texture, or shine, a wider lapel, or a bit of a shoulder pad.

Your goal is to elongate and balance your figure by accentuating your top half. Don't wear long tops that cover your rear end. This will shorten your legs and draw the eye to your bottom half. Do choose tops that sit above the hip and give you a waistline.

Try a structured jacket with interesting details or prints that will direct attention to the top half of your body. Look for jackets that have structure, give you a waistline, and sit above the hip. This will provide a bit of structure to the shoulder area, making your bottom half appear smaller in comparison.

Embellished or embroidered tops are great for centering the focus on your slim upper body. Scarves, earrings. and necklaces are also fabulous attention-grabbers, keeping the eye of the beholder at eye level with you! Play down the effect by keeping your skirt or pants simple and unadorned. No booty bling, bedazzling, or patch and flap back pockets!

Diminish the fuller-on-the-bottom challenge with a dark bootcut trouser and pointy shoes to elongate the leg. Bootcut styles or a slim flare provide a one-two punch as they draw the eye away from your fullest part and the volume at the hemline balances out your hips, making them appear perfectly proportioned.

Lastly, shop for A-line skirts and faux wrap dresses to accentuate your small waistline.

TAILORING TIP: Often women who are fuller on the bottom struggle to find pants that fit both their booty and their waistline. The first line of defense is to shop for the "curvy" fit. If that still leaves a gap that could fit your flip phone, head to the tailor to nip in the waist for a well tailored, professional fit.

FULLER IN THE MIDDLE

If you are fuller in the middle, let's just accentuate the narrowest part of your midsection by moving the focal point up with an empire waist and pulling the attention away from the liability. Again, bring the eye up to your beautiful face by highlighting the neckline with stunning jewelry.

If you have a slim lower body and carry weight around your middle, your goal is to minimize your midsection by highlighting your shoulders and legs.

Opt for a top with structure to balance the middle. A button-front jacket creates a long vertical line. Look for a one or two-button fitted jacket with a stance that hits above the natural waistline. A flowy but not oversized top that falls vertically is the best way to deemphasize your midsection. Try a swing coat. A swing coat will be incredibly flattering on you!

A shift dress lies just far enough away from the body to conceal any problem areas. Look for dresses with substantial fabrications cut with tailored styling and smart details to carve out (or cover up) your middle.

On the bottom, look for pants that rise a bit higher with Lycra or "fit panels" to avoid the dreaded muffin-top. For a skirt, try a high-waisted circle skirt. The waistband will hit at the smallest part of the torso and flare out over the stomach.

Don't forget the all-important shapers that can rake in and contain just about anything. There are three options for controlling your fuller-in-the-middle. You can attack from the top down, meaning wearing an over-the-head shaper that either fits over or under your bra and is tucked into your pants. Or you can attack from the bottom up with pull-up shapers that finish high under the bra line. Finally, you can engage a full-blown attack by wearing a full shaper. These are particularly flattering when donning a dress!

TAILORING TIP: Many women with full figures have shapely legs, so get your dress hemmed a bit shorter to show those gams off!

SHAPELY

You're an hourglass! Congrats to you! Your goal is to highlight your curves, not hide them. Emphasize your smaller waistline with a belted jacket or sweater to play up your curves. Look for items that follow your natural curves and accent the narrowness of your waistline.

Do NOT hide in shapeless garments! A single breasted blazer creates a waistline and a strong V shape from the neckline down. You'll look great in a wrap dress; the v-neck is ultra-flattering to your bust and the wrap detail highlights the curve between your waist and hips.

Choose classic sheaths with fitted waists to enhance your classically Marilyn Monroe form. Look for adjustable-waist styles for the best fit. A pencil skirt accentuates your curves and will smooth out your thighs. Try wide-leg pants with a belted waist. The upside of belted pants? You can be sure they'll fit perfectly at the waist.

TAILORING TIP: Shapely girls come in all heights - be sure your lengths are correct. Check with the tailor to measure and adjust the sleeves and your skirt/dress length to fit and flatter your body scale.

NOT SHAPELY

Fitted sheaths and classic shifts work well with your shape. An empire waist or simple A-line skirt will help to create some curves. Don't attempt to wear clothing that doesn't fit your chest or tush as you'll look like you are playing dress-up.

Do use substantial fabrications with texture or patterns to help create volume. Layer whenever possible and try asymmetrical hemlines as this creates movement and depth. Use scarves to add color and interest, lucky you as you can use those huge scarves that most women do not know what to do with! Check out my scarf tutorial in a later chapter. Lastly, shop for something sexy that shows a little skin!

TAILORING TIP: Just because you are not curvy doesn't mean you don't deserve a tailor! When in doubt, tailor it out! Boxy jackets and baggy pants are not the way to go for you. Tailor them down, show that you care and are well-appointed!

PETITES

Are you vertically challenged? While you may not be able to change the cards you were dealt, the right clothing and accessories can actually help you appear taller than you are. We are going to do a deep dive here as the percentage of women who are petite is quite high! So let's ditch the 6-inch platform shoes and talk about a few ways to fake those extra inches without breaking the bank, or your ankles. Between us girlfriends, let me tell you that you just might have the right items already living in your closet. Let's begin with opening your closet doors, mixing things up, visiting your tailor and maybe shopping for a few accessories to create the illusion.

First off, be mindful of your proportions. As a petite person, it's crucial that your clothing fits properly. All of your clothing and accessories must be kept in proportion with your figure, not allowing any one thing to overpower you. Be sure not to defer to draping as that can sometimes accentuate the liability. Blazer shoulder seams need to fit perfectly so you don't look like you have hand-me-downs. Your sleeve length has to hit exactly at your wrist bone. Try not to wear capris, they cut your calves midway, shortening the legs. Wear cropped pants instead, with the hemline at the ankle.

Wearing different colors top and bottom divides a person's body into separate segments. Monochromatic outfits elongate one's shape. Try one color from head to toe – just pull items out of your closet by color and see what starts to shape up. The monochromatic look creates an uninterrupted visual vertical line. Don't just limit this look to the color black ladies! Try your other neutrals as well – navy, brown, tan, red if you dare! The trick to monochromatic dressing is to keep each silhouette crisp and tailored.

Want longer looking legs? Move your waist-line up. Choose high-waisted skirts or pants to create the illusion you're taller by elongating your lower body. Always be sure to make the elevated waist visible by tucking in a well-fitting blouse, or opting for a slightly shorter top.

Vertical lines – the oldest trick in the book! Vertical lines orient the eye to look up and down, which has a lengthening effect. How to create multiple vertical lines in one outfit? Let me count the ways: buttons down the front of a blouse, sweater, jacket or coat, v-neck as opposed to round neck tops, long jacket lapels that sit low with a one-button stance, well-pressed pants with front creases, and long necklaces with a heavier pendant.

Play with the hemlines. Go either long or short – avoid calf-length and knee-lengths. If you have great legs, a higher hemline will make your gams look even longer. Asymmetrical hems will work in your favor, as your legs will look as long as the shortest point on a skirt or a dress. Wear v-necks and embrace the décolletage (within reason). Tops with a deeper neckline give the illusion of a longer, leaner torso and neck and create a vertical line, while crew necks and scoop necks create a horizontal line.

Chop your hair. Long hair drags petite women down, while shorter hair does the opposite. Showing off your shoulders and neckline will make your frame look tall and proud. Pump up your hair volume – I am not talking a beehive here, but a bit of a topknot or flirty layers will do wonders!

Wear nude shoes that match your skin-tone, as they will visually extend the leg. Opt for a low cut vamp – the front area where it cuts across the top of your foot – the closer to the toes, the longer the leg looks. Shoes with ankle straps are the enemy because they visually bisect the leg. Round-toe shoes can have a shortening effect, while pointed flats and pumps lengthen your leg line. Keeping your shoes and hosiery in the same color range makes it more difficult for the eye to distinguish where the leg ends and the foot begins, resulting in longer looking legs.

Finally, look at your accessories. Hit delete on the over-sized shoulder bag. Keeping your accessories appropriately scaled to your body size is a must. You don't want the bag to be wearing you. Shop for smaller cross-body bags, clutches, and small top-handle totes.

Opt for long, draping accessories (drape doesn't mean bulk). Use long scarves that you can knot many times so they lay vertically centered on your torso. Shop for longer necklaces that drape down your front. Use accessories that draw the eye up and down as opposed to congregating widely around your neckline.

When it comes to belts, vertically challenged women should always opt for a skinny version so it can define your natural waist in the most flattering way. A thick belt will cut you in half causing you to look shorter because of the heavy horizontal line.

Tailoring Tip: Don't assume you are a petite in every store! No two stores abide by the same size scale. Always try on both petite and regular sizes in the same garment when you are on the edge.

Bonus Tailoring Tip: Don't assume that you are a petite on the top and the bottom! You might be a petite top and a regular bottom or vice versa. This can be extra challenging because in many department stores the petite and regular departments might be miles from one another, even on different floors!

"Doreen's professional persistence and exemplary follow-up are what make her such an outstanding businesswoman. She is tremendous at making her clients feel comfortable about defining their desired outcome by taking them through the process of a pre-appointment questionnaire, a free 30-minute phone consult, and requesting photos in advance.

By the time we reached our first meeting we were well acquainted and I was comfortable, excited and well versed in the process, making the outcome even more remarkable! She was on my team before I even hired her! " KT

More Body Hangups

sometimes laughter
is the best medicine

FLABBY ARMS Wear tops with ¾ sleeves. That still gives you plenty of skin that can be accessorized with some arm candy and voila – the observer's eye goes right to the bracelets!

CHICKEN NECK Oh for goodness sake, just dust a little mineral powder on on and buy a new traffic-stopping necklace. Bling always outshines creases!

CANKLES Do not wear shoes with ankle straps as that creates a horizontal line accentuating the wide part of your ankle. Instead choose an open top shoe with a deeper V down to the pointy toe, thereby elongating the leg.

BUNIONS Wear shoes made of material that stretches, such as quality leather or grosgrain. Need a bit more stretch? Fill a ziplock bag with water, place it where you need bunion breathing room and put the shoes in the freezer overnight – as the ice expands the bunion sweet spots are created!

BLUE HAIR Change hairdressers. The Earth will not stop spinning if you try a new hairdresser!

CROWS FEET Check out the anti-aging aisle at CVS, how do you spell billion-dollar industry?

FLAT CHEST
Wear embellished or ruffled tops to add volume.

SHORT LEGS
Dress in monotones from head to toe and finish the look with pointy toe shoes.

BIG HIPS
Buy a pair of flare pants to balance the hipline.

My goodness, how did the list of body hang-ups get so long?

Time to clean the slate, move forward and remember… you are beautiful!

The Black Story

Can you even recognize the black foundational pieces here?

Play the layering game with asymmetrical feminine silk fabrics that achieve fluidity but don't add bulk! Trying to disguise the rear view? Look for stylish tops that are long in the back yet shorter in the front to show off thinner legs. BTW – I could have all sorts of 'fuller-in-the-middle' stuff going on here, but it would be completely disguised. Use style as a tool to create the illusion!

CHAPTER 3

What's In Your Closet?
Must I Open the Doors

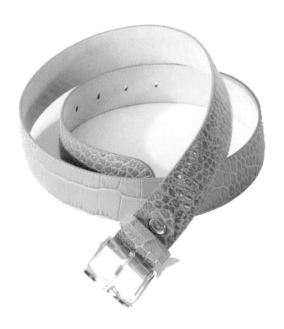

Women only wear 15% of what's in their closet.

Can you imagine? Why then do we hoard the other 85%?

Follow along with me for a moment. I want you to close your eyes and visualize your closet. Now think about how you FEEL when you look at it.

Visualize the space, or the lack thereof, the assorted hangers, the plastic bags, the shoe boxes, the piles of workout clothes, dog walking clothes, laundry, and dry cleaning.

Does it look like this...

Can you imagine if you entered your favorite boutique only to find that it was set up like your closet? Filled with random hangers, completely disorganized, inventory not sectioned by season, cramped clothing and plastic dry cleaning bags mixed in – shall I continue? I am certain you understand the visual difference between how a store displays their inventory and how your clothing is "displayed" in your closet. It should be one in the same: organized, shoppable, and pleasing to your eye so you are enthused and inspired when you swing open the doors.

Wouldn't you prefer it to look like this?

It is completely possible for your closet to be an intuitive, inspirational source of joy. You should look forward to throwing open those doors and selecting all things that fit, flatter, and speak to your authentic style. This is your wardrobe after all. Just like the theatre, this is your costume, your "personal message" about what role you play in life.

Oftentimes when I am standing with a client in the shadow of her closet, we talk about not only where she wants to be in the next phase, but just as importantly, where she was in her previous phases. Who she was, how she dressed, where she frequented, and even how she felt when she dressed a certain way. Women will often pull something out from a decade ago and tell a story about why they bought it, where they bought it, where they wore it and even why they stopped wearing it. Believe it or not, the closet, and the history it holds, is the first step to reinventing your look. There are no doubt fabulous things hiding in your closet from your past that can be reintroduced to your future!

Let me share a client story with you.

When we are in the getting-to-know-each-other phase, I often request that clients send me a picture of their closet. I had a woman respond, "Do the doors have to be open? I thought that was why closets have doors!" Ladies, we cannot build a house if we cannot find the tools in the shed.

I am pretty sure cleaning your closet is not one of the top five items on your to-do list. You might not know where to start, what to save, what to toss, what to tailor or even where to begin!

You have come to the right place! Let's get to it!

First, turn on some music – it just makes everything better.
Second, pour a cup of coffee or a glass of wine depending on the hour (don't be limited by the five o'clock rule).

STEP 1 — Be a good student

Take the time to read my weekly blog posts where I provide great tips on how to save you both time and money by being prepared and organized. This is a great start to get your mind wrapped around both the possibilities and the benefits of a finely-tuned, well-styled wardrobe. Go to www.DoreenDove.com/blog to sign up for the weekly style tips.

"Over the years I have learned that what is important in a dress is the woman who is wearing it."
Yves Saint Laurent

Schedule Closet Time

Grab your calendar. You need to actually schedule closet time on your calendar. I recommend you start with a two-hour block of uninterrupted time. If this is something you have never done and just the thought of it overwhelms you, then by all means do NOT plan to get it all done in one day. Mind you, I can whip through your closet in several hours, but alas, I am the expert and have been doing this for decades. I can spot an outdated, out of style, ill-fitting piece of clothing in an over-crowded, chaotic closet a mile away. You, however are the student now, so let's do this in stages!

Schedule three two-hour blocks of time over the next week or so. Knowing what you are doing is half the battle, learning as you go is the fun part. Once you have gone through a few categories, the balance of the work flows smoother and quicker.

Your wardrobe needs to be evaluated twice a year. With each seasonal change your clothing, shoes, and accessories need to be reassessed for fit, flattery, style, and condition. Did you wear a hole in the knees, do the shoes need polishing, is your handbag a disease zone from being placed on the floor? Don't **ever** do that, by the way! By filtering out the misfits or mistakes you will free up space for something new and exciting. Now that you are on board with the idea, where do you begin?

The Ground Rules

Let's conquer your closet chaos! Your closet should be a source of joy; an intuitive space filled with inspiration and options. You should be able to close your eyes, reach in and select anything (yes anything) and be happy with the choice because it fits, it's flattering, it's in season and it's in style! If there are items in your closet that don't fill those requirements, they are a waste of real estate and they need to move out!

Use the "3 F Rule"
to purge purge purge!

THE "3 F Rule" –
Fit • Flatter • Function

One of the biggest challenges when attacking the wardrobe is figuring out whether it is a closet keeper or not. That is easily determined by applying The 3 F Rule: Fit, Flatter & Function!

FIT (and the Dreaded Ws)

Imagine there is a woman named Sadie whose weight has fluctuated up and down over the past 10 years. She bought new black pants every time she lost weight and new black pants every time she gained weight. She now has 20 pairs of black pants taking over her closet.

How many of you can relate to Sadie's story?
Sadie is obviously not alone – you aren't alone either.

The Dreaded Ws stand for Weight… W.E.I.G.H.T. and Wait… W.A.I.T.

Let's address this challenge of the Dreaded Ws from 2 perspectives. The first perspective is the mental aspect. The mental is the dreaded word weight which always leaves you waiting. Now is the time, not later. Arthur Ashe, a very famous tennis player said:

"One important key to success is self-confidence.
An important key to self-confidence is preparation."

You need to look and feel pretty today, and stop waiting to feel that way tomorrow or six months from now.

The second perspective is taking practical steps towards buying the right type of clothing for your body type (and your weight) so you actually look fabulous in the clothes you put on!

Doreen's tip on sizing: If your weight fluctuates, keep only one size above your current size and one size below.

FLATTER

Flattering means, does it fit: does it need tailoring, is the style current, is it age appropriate, does it even match who you are right now or who you want to be?

Maybe your closet is filled with oldies but goodies. Is it time to re-evaluate your taste? Is an oldie really a goodie? Is the Stevie Nicks look really flattering on you now? How about the bib-front jeans? Oh, and here's a huge category – how many Mr. Rogers cardigans are too many?

Silhouettes that are twice as big as your frame are old news – we've come a long way baby. Stop draping. Fitted is better! It's more flattering, more current, and shows confidence in your style choices. There are styles for all body shapes. When working with clients I always accentuate the assets and disguise the liabilities. We all have our share of both – just learn how to manipulate your wardrobe. After all, the wardrobe that the actor is wearing on stage is disguising her real persona and putting out what she wants you to see.

FUNCTION

If it hasn't seen the light of day in 10 years then I certainly don't think it is going to be the first thing you pull out for your next important event. And if it is not functioning, then it is just a waste of real estate!

Let me share one client story because I can hear what you are thinking, "But Doreen, what about the 'special' things?" One client had an 8 pound sweatshirt that was taking up an entire cubby in her closet (she could have easily had 20 pair of Lululemons in this space) – so I pulled it out and asked her what about this sweatshirt was so special that it had a cubby devoted to it for 20 years. The Fleetwood Mac logo! I bought her a 6 inch shadow box, she cut the logo out and mounted it in the box with a picture of her and her sister at the concert. It now sits on a shelf...OUTSIDE of the closet! (More on keepsakes later.)

Be inspired to have a wardrobe that serves you as opposed to holding you back from being the best version of you. Decide which items have outlived their purpose, which items could be updated with tailoring, and which items should be stored off-season. End result goal: to have a closet full of clothes that fit, flatter, coordinate, and make you look and feel fabulous!

Sort It Out

What do you do with the "unwanteds"? Get them out of the room or closet as you are sorting. If you don't put them in another area away from the good stuff, you may find they have migrated back into your closet, and you've just wasted your time.

Before   Clothes Out

Shoes Out   After

It's also harder to see what you are keeping when there's a lot of clutter. Grab some shopping bags and label them DONATE, CONSIGN, TAILORING, and OUT OF SEASON. Be sure to separate the donation pile from the consignments; donating is a great way to get rid of these things, but if you think they have monetary value you may want to take them to a consignment shop.

The Categories

Some image consultants like to jump in with defining what's wrong with all of the items in your closet. Let's start by saying your closet no doubt is filled with fabulous things, as well as a few not so fabulous. It will be up to you to decide which side of the fence your things are on based on the parameters I describe below.

I want to break it down by category for you – it's much more manageable this way and allows you to work on a category or two at a time (within your two-hour window) and experience real results along the way. This will also allow you to still be able to actually maneuver around your room and get dressed on the days in between!

Here are the categories: pants, skirts, jackets, dresses, sweaters, tops, shoes, and accessories. In general I start with bottoms (pants and skirts), then move to dresses, tops, shoes and finish with accessories.

PANTS

These are usually the hardest item to fit and most women accumulate pants because they "replace" a basic black pant, but never "purge" the pair they are replacing! Usually their thought process behind "replacing" is that they are continually in search of the best-fitting, traffic-stopping pair of black pants on the planet! Sound familiar? Wait until you see how many black pants come out of your closet!

SKIRTS

Women just hold onto skirts in general. This category usually spans 'decades' – yes decades. We find peasant skirts from the Woodstock era (oh maybe it will come back), floor length wool gabardines from the 80's (I was thinking of shortening those), flirty little flower prints with elastic waist-bands – in 3 colors (they were on sale) and schoolgirl plaids (no words necessary). Then when I ask how often they wear skirts, it is about once a month, meaning they don't need fifty skirts in their closet.

JACKETS

Jackets are hard for women to part with for many reasons. Here's the top five: they were expensive, they were part of a suit (bottoms long gone), I was thinking I could get it tailored (4-inch shoulder pads), I was sure it would come back in style (not), I don't know where to donate them (numerous options). With that said, we move right into jackets after pants and skirts because after all – they work so well together! There should be some intentional synergy between your jackets and your pants/skirts.

SUITS

Let's start with the main question here – do you actually wear suits? If the answer is yes, then let us proceed. My preference is to hang the suits as separates. Long gone are the days when we actually wore out our clothing. So if one of the suit pieces (the jacket, skirt or pant) gets worn a bit more often than the others, let's consider that a bonus point for getting those cost-per-wear numbers down. A solid bottom is a solid bottom and can be worn with tweed jackets, sweaters and

even just beautiful blouses. Split up the items – hang pants with pants, skirts with skirts and the jackets with the jackets. This also applies if you are not wearing those corporate suits anymore. No need to give the whole suit away if one of the pieces fits well and works nicely into your wardrobe. Think dark wash jeans, crisp white shirt, a great belt and silver necklace and then top it off with the solid black jacket for a sharp look (way better than topping it off with a frumpy cardigan sweater). Jackets exude confidence and authority, so just go for it!

DRESSES

I call this the "plastic bag category" as there are always numerous dresses either way left or way right in the closet covered in dusty murky dry cleaner bags, some with the bottoms tied (as if they are going to escape). Admittedly, most are special occasion dresses...let's be clear here. Special occasions are the perfect excuse to buy a NEW dress! And in this digital age, who wants someone seeing four pictures of you wearing the same old black glittery dress with the only difference being your hairstyle! So yes, dresses are the next category...bring your sense of humor and your giving heart for this section.

SWEATERS

This is a huge category because of all of the "places" that we can store sweaters and "store" we do! Closets, shelves, boxes, bins, drawers, cedar chests...the list goes on. When I ask a client to gather this category I hear them go upstairs, downstairs, and every place in between. So be prepared for this challenge and I recommend to start this category potentially at the beginning of the day, because it could take a while!

TOPS

These need to be worked on by style. Start with sleeveless and move to short sleeve, then long sleeve blouses and lastly long sleeve woven shirts (meaning those cotton shirts you hate to iron). We'll go into more detail later.

SHOES

This is the perfect category to wind down with because now we know what you own as far as clothing (and what you might need). This is a simple process, pretty clear-cut, but again, may require some hunting and gathering.

ACCESSORIES

Yes this is a category! We'll start with scarves and then move to jewelry and bags. Bring your bravery (to be honest with yourself), your discerning eye (pretend you are actually buying these items today), and your energy (this will be work)! But it will be work with purpose!

Let's begin!

PANTS

Take every pair of pants out of the closet and off the hangers. Toss the junky store hangers. Yes, toss them, they were not part of the price and the stores give them to you to get them the heck out of their way. Save your chubby plastic tube hangers for your heavy winter coat closet.

Stack the pants open-length on the bed by type – dress, casual, and jeans. Then arrange the stacks by color – from white to black (the black stack is historically quite high!)
Within each type and color stack, assess each pant for:

Fit, Flattery & Function

- Are there any tailoring tweaks that might be necessary?
- Do they still have the tags on?
- Are they flattering from the front AND the back?
- Have you worn them in the last 2 years?
- Are the side pockets gaping? They can be sewn closed and the liner removed by the tailor – a cheap fix for smooth sides!

- Is the waist too big?
- Put all items that need to be tailored in the TAILORING pi
- Are they in style or not so much?
- Are they so long so you can only wear them with stilettos so you never wear them?

All pants that are not flattering, out of style or are not being worn go in the DONATE pile.

pants...

All remaining pants need to be hung uniformly on fold-over hangers with the top of the pant on the left and the bottom on the right. The more strategically hung, the better they will stay pressed and crisp. Reintroduce them to the closet left to right from white to black – dress pants to casual pants to jeans. Oftentimes hanging space is at a premium; you can fold the jeans and stack them on a shelf, or purchase a doubler to split the horizontal closet rod into two sections – allowing you to hang pants on the bottom and shirts on the top.

SKIRTS

Take them all off hangers and toss the bad hangers. Pile them open length on the bed by:
Type – casual/dress or short/long depending on your collection.
Color – stacks by color or solids/patterns
Within each type and color stack, assess each skirt for:

Fit, Flattery & Function

- Do they fit – are there any tailoring tweaks that might be necessary?
- Are there buttons missing or are there fussy zippers that cause issues?
- Is the kick pleat too low (can't take stairs) or too high (can't sit like a lady)?
- Are they a frump-ville length so you are never sure whether to wear them with flats or heels? Just decide!
- Put all items that need to be tailored in the TAILORING pile.
- Are they too flowery and flowing to be flattering?
- Are they age appropriate – too young or too old looking for you?
- Were they a hand-me-down and you are keeping them out of guilt?
- Do you only wear them as part of a suit? Stop that! Hang them with skirts and increase your skirt options!

All skirts that are not flattering, out of style or are not being worn go in the DONATE pile.

All remaining skirts need to be hung uniformly on the 4-tier cascading hangers by type. Hang all your short solids together, all short patterns and all long skirts together. That way when you "shop" in your closet for a skirt, you can shop by style. The more strategically hung they are, the quicker your outfit will come together because usually the skirt style dictates the shoe worn with it. Be aware – you are often dressing to match how your feet have to perform that day.

Reintroduce the skirts to the closet near the dresses, as they will need longer hanging space now that they are cascading.

"Doreen is a power house of knowledge when it comes to making women look good, feel fabulous and raising the bar on self-confidence. Having her in my closet was a benefit beyond my imagination. It was amazing to see my clothing before and after she worked her magic. I was so ready to throw them all out and start over! Now I have so much to wear and I get dressed with ease every morning. I can't thank you enough. You provide such a terrific unique service!" JL

JACKETS

Take them all off hangers (toss the bad hangers). Pile them on the bed by type: casual, work blazers, suit jackets, and dressy cocktail jackets.
Within each type assess each jacket for:

Fit, Flattery & Function

- Are these jackets well tailored?
- Can they be buttoned?
- Are the sleeves the correct length?
- Is the length of the jacket correct for your body shape? Remember jackets come in petite, regular, and tall!
- Could you nip in the waist to show off your assets?
- Put all jackets that need to be tailored in the TAILORING pile.
- Are these jackets still stylish?
- Are the shoulder pads as broad as the doorway – might be time to move those to the donate pile.
- Are they too heavy for office-wear? Harris tweeds for example, could be used for fox hunting, but you would sweat to death at your desk!
- Are some of your "obvious" suit jackets (think menswear pinstripes) lonely because the pants are long gone and the jackets are obviously missing their mates? Time to donate…
- Are some of these jackets too old for you – queen mum looking?
- Are any double-breasted and you now realize that double-breasted is not the best style for extra-in-the-middle?
- Have you worn them in the last 2 years?

All that are not flattering, out of style or are not fully functioning members of your wardrobe go in the DONATE pile.

All remaining jackets need to be hung uniformly on the skinny black soft-grip velvet hangers. Hang them left to right, light to dark, inter-mixing the patterns by color. The more strategically hung they are, the better they will stay pressed and crisp and the better you will be able to shop from them!

Any true "outside" jackets should go to an "outside" closet where you keep your outerwear.

"Style is a way to say who you are without having to speak."
Rachel Zoe

DRESSES

Rip off the plastic bags and take them all off the hangers (toss the bad hangers).
Pile them open length on the bed by type: casual, work and cocktail.
Within each type assess each dress for:

Fit, Flattery & Function

- Are these casual dresses age appropriate or do they look like a teen sundress?
- Are these work dresses well-tailored, dress code appropriate, potentially dullsville?
- Are these cocktail dresses over-glittered or as old as the hills?
- Do you still need your prom/wedding dress taking up valuable real estate in your closet?
- Do they fit – are there any tailoring tweaks that might make them more flattering?
- Should the armholes be brought up higher so no "stuff" shows under your arms?
- Could you nip in the waist or adjust the length to show off your assets?
- Put all dresses that need to be tailored in the TAILORING pile.
- Are they flattering from the front AND the back?
- Are they in style or not so much?
- Have you worn them in the last 2 years?
- Do they still have the tags on?
- Do you feel pretty when you put them on?

All that are not flattering, out of style or are not fully functioning members of your wardrobe go in the DONATE pile.

All remaining dresses need to be hung uniformly on the skinny black soft grip velvet hangers. The more strategically hung they are, the better they will stay pressed and crisp and the better you will be able to shop from them! There should be no need for plastic dry cleaning bags now. If you have "true keepers" please consider picking up breathable long garment bags and try to store them in an off season closet so they don't crowd your daily duds and aren't crushed themselves.

Reintroduce your dresses to the closet left to right, from sleeveless to short sleeve to long sleeve to evening dresses.

SWEATERS

Take every sweater out of the closet, the cubbies, the boxes, the vacuum sealed bags, the cedar closets. From under the bed and the kids' rooms. Catch my drift here – no doubt you have sweaters everywhere!

Let's do this once and done.

First, you need to determine if a sweater is winter or spring. You really should only have one season at a time at your fingertips. The out-of-season batch should be dry cleaned or washed before storing because moths love dirty clothes, most especially the oils around the necklines.

For our purposes, let's presume you are working on one season of sweaters at a time. Stack the sweaters on the bed by type. I recommend you start with only one type at a time. Start with cardigans as they tend to be the biggest, floppiest and oftentimes the most outdated as we tend to say, "Oh I will just keep this for house-lounging-days..." But alas they are never moved to the lounge chair and seriously how many days do you spend lounging around in grandpa's sweaters? (Do you even have a lounging chair?)

Within each type and color stack assess each sweater for:

Fit, Flattery & Function
• Repairs required, moth nibbles, buttons missing, seams opening up?
• Are they in shape or out of shape, possibly stretched beyond reason?
• Do they fit, too small to button, too big so you look like a linebacker minus the pads?
• Are the "V"s so low your belt is showing?
• Is the "knit one purl one" so bulky you can be mistaken for the Michelin man?
• Are the sleeves so long you won't need gloves?
• Most sweater fit issues cannot be corrected with tailoring - time to donate.
• Do they smell like mothballs or a cedar closet? Get those dry cleaned – maybe twice!
• Are they functioning or dysfunctional?

Do you have soooo many sweaters that you couldn't possibly rotate them once on an annual basis? Have you ever heard of "FIFO"? First in, first out.

What to purge? That will become obvious when you find that your stack of black v-neck sweaters is higher than your stack of bedsheets in the linen closet. You just don't need 12 of those. Pick the top two favorites and donate the rest.

To Fold or Not To Fold?

If you aren't a folder, then hanging those T-shirts, jerseys and light weight sweaters will work better for you. My personal preference is to hang this entire top category. It makes your inventory options visible and keeps the wrinkles from taking over. You need to work with the space and storage you have, which may mean purchasing a few closet accessories to control the chaos.

sweaters...

If you are a folder and have shelves or drawers for them, then categorize them and decide by quantity and convenience whether they go in a drawer or on a shelf. When folding, make the items consistent so they look nice and stack well. Pick up a folding board to use with shirts and sweaters. You simply fold around the board, pull it out and voila! Your stacks look like J. Crew and now you can work there part time, receive a discount and buy MORE sweaters!

There are also vertical shelf dividers that clip on the shelf to keep your stacks from mingling with one another once you turn the lights off! Without those, they may fall over and get messy again, and you're back to square one.

Another great option is buying mesh cubes for sweaters. By keeping them folded and stacked high, they can be brought down from the shelf so you can peruse through that selection only.

TOPS

Take every top out of the closet and off the hangers. Toss the junky hangers. Stack each top on the bed by type then arrange the stacks by color – from white to black.

T-shirts or jerseys - (think casual) divide by sleeve length.
True blouses, divide by sleeveless, short sleeve and long sleeve.
Woven shirts (think menswear with collars) - most of these are long sleeve unless you work for UPS!

Within each type and color stack assess each top for:

Fit, Flattery & Function

- **T-shirts & jerseys:** Assess their overall condition and donate or dump those with underarm stains and/or tattered edges, or if they are belly baring, faded beyond stylish, or just in quantities to outfit a small army. Downsize and move on.
- **Assess the sleeveless for fit:** Are you actually showing underarm carnage or side boob? Then they don't fit - donate.
- **Assess the short sleeve for flattery:** If the last short sleeve blouse you saw came with a pocket protector, then they are out of style - donate.
- **Assess the woven shirts for function:** If you don't own an iron, don't know how to iron, or don't want to pay to have those shirts dry cleaned, then you are never going to wear them because they will always be wrinkled. Get the inventory down to a bare minimum which should include a crisp white shirt, and donate the rest to the kids painting class. Wrinkled smocks always welcome there! The next time you shop for a woven menswear shirt, make sure the label says non-iron and you will actually wear the shirt.

SHOES

Again this is a category that should definitely be separated by season with the off-season inventory stored out of site. The only inventory in your closet should be the current season. My favorite shoe storage is in clear plastic bins known miraculously as boot boxes! You can easily fit 2 pair of boots in each and when it is time for those to be freed, you can side stack about a dozen pair of sandals in that one box. By using the clear boxes you can easily locate those special off-season sandals for the cruise of a lifetime.

Then take all your shoes out of the closet, line them up by type, stand back and say holy moly...I have too many shoes. Go ahead, say it – it will be a turning point for you.

Needless to say, perform the fit, flatter and function ritual on all shoes before packing them away.

Fit, Flattery & Function

• Have your pumps been discolored from pumping the gas pedal?
• Are they chewed up by cobblestones?
• Do they need new heels; something called shoe polish or maybe just a ride to the dump?
• Did you buy a pair to replace a pair but somehow still have both?
• Here's a big one – are they COMFORTABLE?

No more justifying and rationalizing, move on and perform a shoe cleanse.

Move through by type, start with sneakers for example, and ask yourself how many do I really need? If you have too many, purge the old smelly worn out pair (those just go to the dump). Go through each subsequent shoe category the same way, sandals that are torn, high heels that got caught in the grates and so on. Check the tops and the bottoms, you never know who is look-ing! Here's a good one. I was sitting in a room filled with corpo-rate women at a networking breakfast. The woman in front of me was impeccably dressed and accessorized. Then she crossed her leg and exposed a big round red sticker with an '8' on it – not the lucky ball 8 mind you – it was the size sticker from a local discount shoe store!

When you reintroduce the keepers back into your closet, be creative! Here is a linen closet that we took over one client's house because her closet was too small and dark to properly display her shoe affliction. Sheets out - stilettos in!

shoes...

If you are "shelving" shoes, put your clunky shoes low on the floor, your flats together a few shelves up, then your pumps. When the shelves get higher than eye level stack the heels out so you can visually see the selection. Do NOT keep the boxes. They were not part of the price.

If you have special occasion shoes or you sprung for some Loubi's, then buy a few clear plastic shoe boxes to display them proudly. Shoes hidden in cardboard shoe boxes never come out to play and they become the forgotten footwear!

ACCESSORIES | JEWELRY

If your jewelry box is filled with a collection of peace signs and beaded kid treasures then yes – you need to shop for accessories. The list could include a fashion ring, a silver or gold cuff bracelet, a selection of necklaces – short, long, chunky, delicate, mixed metals and colored stones. Jewels can be bought at all price points and your collection will build over time. Go for classic but infuse some trendy pieces when they are on sale. The key is to start noticing trends, just as I said at the beginning. Start noticing jewelry on others, on mannequins, in your promotional emails and style magazines. Before you know it you will be bumping up your accessory drawer at all price points like it was your business and your "authentic style" will thank you!

SCARVES

What is better than surrounding yourself in a soft supple colorful scarf? They are my favorite accessory as they quickly finish an outfit with the flip of a loop, polish off your neutral zone, and frame your beautiful face with color, texture & shine!

Choose fabrics like cotton, rayon, silk, viscose, linen or a mix of many. Build your collection with solids, patterns, long, short, big and small. This accessory is a year-round game changer.

Take a look at how I tamed this huge beautiful scarf - you can bet I will tie this differently every time I wear it. With a few twists, turns and knots you too will soon be styling your scarves like a pro!

- Start by twisting away
- Loop in the front and cross in the back
- Pull the front loop down to expose your bling
- Loop both ends up and through front loop
- Now start knotting the long pieces
- VOILÀ - I have created that all important vertical line!

HANDBAGS

When was the last time you performed a bag assessment? A purse is more than an accessory – it is a statement, an investment, and a daily companion.

Seriously, what do you hold more often than your bag? You carry it every day, so it has to be versatile, comfortable and good looking. It has to be able to endure being hung, dropped, stretched, stuffed, and occasionally tossed in the backseat, as well as thick-skinned in order to take verbal abuse when you can't find something inside.

Head into your closet, take all your bags out, fish through each for cash, line them up by type, step back and say "oh my" and then get a garbage bag! These are the items that go in the garbage/donate bag: If it is so small it looks like a childs bag, if it is so big your child could be inside, if it is in disrepair beyond hope, if the inside has more mineral powder than your actual makeup bag, if it smells like a banana peel, if it is one color on the top and some color resembling dirt on the bottom, if it is a style more appropriate for Daisy Duke or if it is just plain really ugly. Your handbag is a reflection of you, step it up!

The Black Story

One blouse, so many options! Pick a pattern that matches your frame, small prints for smaller frames and larger prints for larger frames. When I look at my clients' closets, it is quickly apparent whether they are attracted to florals or geometrics, but oftentimes they don't even realize what's trending in their own wardrobe. Decide which you like, which looks better on you and stay on trend, otherwise you will end up with one-shot-wonders in your closet. Items that you purchased on a whim that never get invited out of the closet!

The Well Dressed Closet

Let's define the ground rules around making your closet well dressed
with closet accessories including fabulous hangers, shoeboxes and keepsakes.

Hangers

First and foremost, those random plastic hangers that
came with your purchase or the lovely wire hangers that
came from the drycleaner were NOT part of the price! Just
like the shoebox that came with the shoes – again NOT
part of the price! There is no value in random, chunky,
plastic rainbow colored hangers or dust bunny collecting

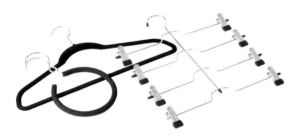

cardboard boxes! Let's get with the program – the absolute best hangers out there are the skinny velvet
hangers in black. Unless you have a walk-in closet the size of Texas, the plastics are not what you want
to have in there. Consistency of the hangers is a critical component to an organized closet! Buy them
and be once and done! You will fit twice as many garments in the same space!

Shoeboxes

Again, not part of the price so start breaking them down for cardboard recycling!

I recommend you own at least 2 CLEAR boot boxes for off
season storage. One of these 22 x 14 x 5 inch boxes can hold a
dozen pair of sandals stacked sideways. By always using clear
boxes you can see what is stored, just in case you need your Jack
Rogers for Acapulco in January. Then stash the box under the
bed, on the top shelf of the closet or even in the attic till the
snow melts. This leaves lovely display room for your winter shoes
and boots. When the time comes to switch seasons, you just use
the same boxes. You may need one or two more for the storage
of winter shoes due to the bulk.

*"Doreen has managed to control my clothing chaos throughout my entire
house! I travel weekly and the biggest a-ha moment I had was when she
set-up a space for my carry-on items. Every time I switched luggage, my
items were all over the place and hard to find. I now have them in one drawer,
contained and ready to go. Doreen also helped me organize my wardrobe
and spruce up my style. I can see what I have and there is a place for everything. She created a look-book for me for several different color combinations
which makes packing a breeze. I would highly recommend Doreen to anyone
who needs help with their clothing, closet and style." AP*